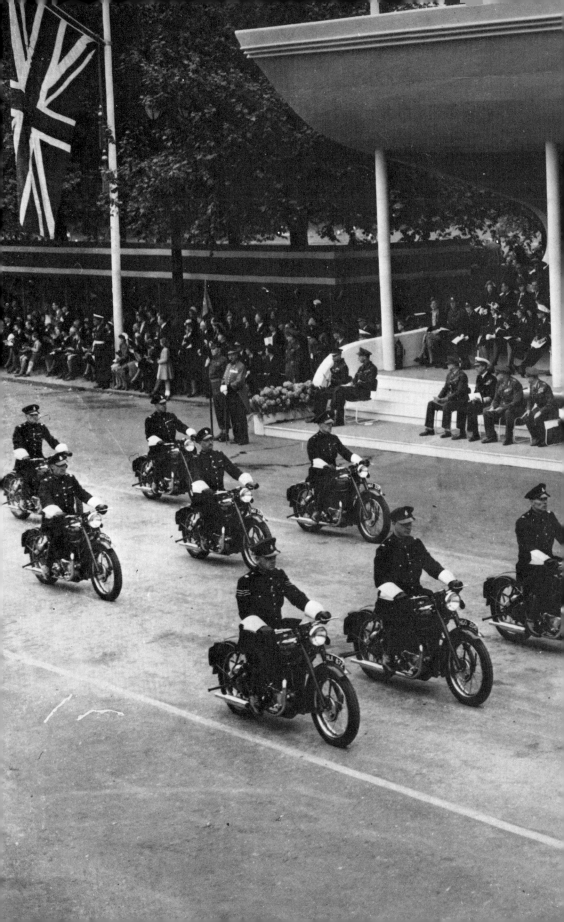

The VICTORY PARADE
London, 8th June 1946

A very famous Triumph picture. Knowing that the Metropolitan Police would be in the Victory Parade on their new Speed Twins the author phoned a London press agency a few days before and asked them to see what shots they could get of the police 'posse'. Little did he imagine that they would come up with something like this. It was one of those lucky breaks that one occasionally gets in the publicity business. Obviously, wide use was made of the picture. It featured on the front cover of the 1947 Triumph catalogue after an artist had skilfully added some colour – the original being black and white, of course. Framed, it has hung in the Reception Room at the Meriden Works since 1946.

The photograph shows the saluting base in the Mall and in addition to Their Majesties the King and Queen, many famous wartime leaders, British and Allied, will be recognised, Mr Churchill is third from the right in the group of four to the right of the dais.

Contents

Acknowledgements

In a book of this type there is nothing more valuable than to have the co-operation of people who were actually part of the story. So I must firstly thank two good friends and ex-colleagues Jack Wickes and Don Brown for their help. Jack, after working alongside Edward Turner for more than thirty years was able to supply from first hand much of the material dealing with the early days of Turner and Triumph Engineering. Don Brown, a top executive for many years in our USA operation has produced some equally absorbing reading about Triumph's biggest market.

Edward Turner himself expressed great interest in the work at one time and promised every assistance but sadly passed away before this became possible. Fortunately his long serving secretary, Nan Plant, was able to produce many interesting facts, figures and photographs, and I am indeed grateful to her as also for her help with the typing.

Then I must tender a somewhat belated thank you to the Triumph Engineering board of the day who authorised the use of company files, photographs and other material. Thanks also go to Jim Alves, Norman Hyde, John Nelson, Alex Scobie, Tyrell Smith and Les Williams for confirmation of dates and details.

I offer my apologies to those copyright holders of some of the older photographs where all efforts to contact them have failed.

Finally I must express my appreciation to the publishers for their forebearance over the years during which this book has done several U-turns due to upheavals in the industry and other circumstances beyond anyone's control.

Writing the book has to some extent been a labour of love because Triumph was a unique and exciting company to work for. We used to say that there were three ways to do a job 'the right way, the wrong way, and the Triumph way'. I hope I have managed to write this book 'the Triumph way'.

Ivor Davies

Preface

Let us say right at the outset that this book is not a definitive history of the Triumph motorcycle although some of the material published here will add to that rich and interesting story. There is a thread of history running through it but it is in reality an illustrated story of Triumph. It divides into two parts the dividing line being roughly the end of World War 2.

Part One is to some extent historical with material from the files of the old Triumph Cycle Company. This leads into the setting up of Triumph Engineering, the introduction of the Speed Twin and World War 2.

Part Two deals with the area in which the author was involved during his long employment with the company in advertising and sales promotion, which of course includes the competition field. Regrettably, the meticulous photographic records of the late forties and fifties were not maintained, so that the bulk of the pictures are from this period. However it was fortunately the most exciting, successful and profitable period of Triumph history.

After this we reprint in full a report on the Japanese motorcycle industry prepared by Edward Turner in 1960. This should dispel for ever the myth that we were not warned.

Finally, there is a picture gallery comprising a wide assortment of photographs from the Triumph archives. Not many of these have been published before and we feel sure that Triumph enthusiasts will find them of considerable interest.

Chapter One

A brief history

The Triumph motorcycle has a long and honourable history which has been told many times in the press and elsewhere. I do not propose to repeat it in this book but for the benefit of those who are not familiar with it, a brief summary here may be of assistance in relating the various incidents and periods dealt with in other parts of the book.

For a motorcycle as British as the Triumph, it is remarkable, to say the least, that it originated in the mind and efforts of a young German, Siegfried Bettmann who came to this country in 1884. After a brief period working for Kelly's, the directory publishers, Bettmann started his own import-export business in London in 1885. The bicycle boom was on at this time and Bettmann exported Birmingham-made bicycles with a 'Bettmann' label. However, in 1886 he changed this to 'Triumph', reckoning it would be more easily understood by his European customers. In 1887 he was joined by another young German, Mauritz Schulte, an engineer. A year later he moved from London to Coventry, then the centre of the bicycle industry, where he rented a small factory in order to set up his own manufacturing facility.

Schulte was very interested in the developing motor industry and in 1902 he fitted a Belgian $2\frac{1}{4}$ hp Minerva engine into a Triumph bicycle – the first Triumph motorcycle was born. By 1905 the company had designed and made its own 3hp engine and from this there grew a range of models which, thanks to sound design and good quality, soon built up a reputation for reliability second to none. It has even been said that Triumph rescued the motorcycle from oblivion by proving that a roadworthy reliable machine could be produced. The nickname 'Trusty Triumph' came into being at this time.

During the Great War, Triumph were major suppliers of motorcycles to both the British and Allied forces and after the war continued to offer a wide range of single cylinder models and also a selection of sidecars to suit. These were not very inspired designs, being developed from those of pre-war days. However they were well made and probably as good as and

The first Triumph motorcycle was produced in 1902 and this much published picture of it appeared in a Triumph Cycle Co Ltd booklet of 1924, which also stated that it had a Minerva (Belgian) engine of $2\frac{1}{4}$ hp. The illustration is retouched to such an extent that its photographic origin is virtually lost and details are vague. It is therefore interesting to compare it with an actual Triumph motorcycle of the same period. There is a distinct family likeness. This other one has a JAP engine of 293cc (70 x 76mm), automatic inlet valve and a single tank-mounted lever which 'controls simultaneously the throttle and the ignition advance'. Various makes of engine were used experimentally at this time and this JAP-engined model of 1903 vintage is preserved in the National Motor Museum in Beaulieu. It is very probably the oldest Triumph motorcycle in existence.

possibly better than anything else offered at the time. The 4 valve ohv Model 'R' (Ricardo) caused a stir with its advanced design of engine but the bicycle and running gear surrounding it were stock side-valve, right down to the dummy belt rim rear brake.

This state of affairs continued up to the early thirties when financial problems beset the company as they did many others in these depression years. However in 1932 designer Val Page joined the company from Ariel and for the 1933/4 season produced a completely new range of good looking modern motorcycles – the old, somewhat vintage looking Triumph had gone for ever.

However, even these new models failed to reverse the financial difficulties of the company and a decision was made to cease the manufacture of motorcycles altogether in order to concentrate on the car side. At this point, Jack Sangster, who had revived the Ariel marque a few years before, stepped in and bought up the Triumph motorcycle business and transferred from Ariel, as Chief Designer and Managing Director, Edward Turner. Turner was the brilliant designer of the Ariel Square Four and the Red Hunter range.

From that time on, Triumph never looked back. Turner's Speed Twin, which came out in 1937, set a new standard throughout the world and was widely copied. It was followed by a galaxy of superb motorcycles which included the Tiger 100, Thunderbird, Trophy, T110 and Bonneville, which brought fame and prosperity to the Meriden factory, and it is this period in Triumph history with which this book is mainly concerned.

Edward Turner

John Y. Sangster

Siegfried Bettman

The 'BIG THREE' of Triumph

In the 80 years from 1885 to 1965, three men stand out as the real controllers of Triumph destiny: Siegfried Bettmann, who founded the company, John Y. Sangster and Edward Turner. There were plenty of others who made significant contributions but these were the 'Big Three'. They actually 'overlapped' for a brief period when Bettmann was invited to become Chairman of Sangster's new Triumph Engineering Co Ltd in 1936. Bettmann was a businessman and financier rather than a motorcycle engineer, but he started the company, gave it it's name and ran it successfully for a very long time. The Sangster family had controlled the Ariel company from way back in the nineties but it was 'Mr. Jack' who rescued it from bankruptcy in the depression of the twenties. He did the same for Triumph, a few years later. Edward Turner was an engineer and designer employed by Sangster, first at Ariel and then at Triumph, whose motorcycles brought great success to both these companies. He died in 1973.

14

Chapter Two

The first Triumph motorcycles

Although the first Triumph motorcycle appeared in 1902, it was from 1905 that the Triumph reputation for reliability and performance began to build up. In this year the company produced, for the first time, its own engine made entirely in its own factory. This was a single cylinder side-valve 78 x 76 mm (363 cc) for which 3hp was claimed at 1500 rpm.

This little engine, with its mainshaft running on ball bearings and with optional magneto ignition, was beautifully made and put together and this showed on the road.

By 1907 the engine had increased to 82 x 86 mm (453 cc), then to 84 x 84 mm (476 cc) in 1908. In 1910 it grew again to 85 x 85 mm (499 cc) and in 1914 to 85 x 97 mm (550 cc) and there it stuck. The 363 cc was classified as 3hp, the three 500's as $3\frac{1}{2}$ hp and the 550 cc as 4 hp.

The significant thing in this period was that although a 70 x 76mm (292 cc or $2\frac{1}{2}$ hp model) was listed alongside the new all-Triumph 3 hp in 1906, the $2\frac{1}{2}$ hp looked like a bicycle with a motor in it but the 3 hp was definitely a motorcycle. This was the parting of the ways and the $2\frac{1}{2}$ hp did not appear in the 1907 catalogue. The true motorcycle had been born, with its lower frame and saddle as the need for pedalling diminished and, once the adjustable pulley and the three-speed hub were introduced, then pedals were on the way out. By the time World War 1 had been going for a short time, the Model 'H' came along with a separate Sturmey Archer countershaft 3-speed gearbox mounted behind the engine and the format of the modern motorcycle could be seen.

Browsing through the early catalogues is an interesting experience, particularly for someone like myself who has undoubtedly produced more Triumph catalogues in his time than anyone else.

Today the catalogue is a simple selling tool which illustrates the motorcycle in superb colour, includes a technical specification, some chat and a pretty girl or two – and that's it.

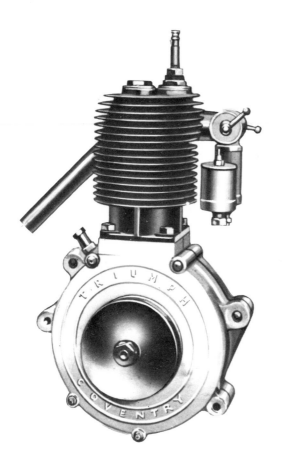

1905 engine, 78 x 76 mm (363cc).
Made entirely in the Triumph works.
Claimed to be the first successful engine
with ball bearing 'mains'.

3 hp model 1906 with accumulator
ignition.

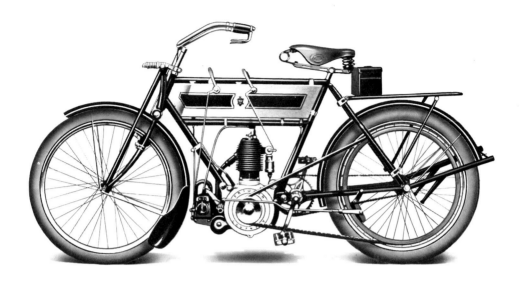

3 hp model 1906 with magneto ignition (£5 extra).

Triumph Motor Cycle.

2½ h.p.

HANDLE-BAR CONTROL.

This Motor Bicycle has gained a reputation for speed, hill-climbing, and reliability; we introduced this machine last year, and the results have been so satisfactory that we have altered it only in a few minor details.

Telegraphic Code: Triumph Motor Bicycle, 2½ h.p. - - - MOTOPLATE.

10

$2\frac{1}{2}$ hp model 1906, still has that primitive look about it.

3½ hp model 1908, a lower frame and beginning to look like a real motorcycle.

1908 engine, 84 x 84 mm (476cc). Who said 'square' engines were a modern development.

The incredible Triumph spring fork of 1908 with a ball bearing pivot at the base of the steering head. A similar fork was still being used in the twenties, for some models.

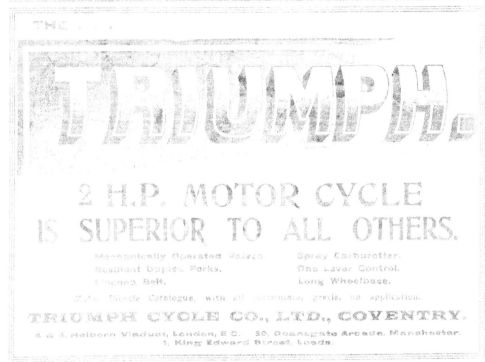

THE ...

TRIUMPH

2 H.P. MOTOR CYCLE
IS SUPERIOR TO ALL OTHERS.

Mechanically Operated Valves.　　　Spray Carburetter.
Resilient Duplex Forks.　　　One Lever Control.
Linened Belt.　　　Long Wheelbase.

Motor Bicycle Catalogue, with all particulars, gratis, on application.

TRIUMPH CYCLE CO., LTD., COVENTRY.

4 & 5, Holborn Viaduct, London, E.C.　　30, Deansgate Arcade, Manchester.
5, King Edward Street, Leeds.

A Triumph advertisement from the very first issue of 'The Motor Cycle' dated 31st March 1903 (price twopence). Prior to and during World War 2, the slogan was 'The World's Pre-eminent Motor Cycle'. From 1946 on we adopted 'The Best Motorcycle in the World' — the message has always been the same, right from 1903.

In the early days of the century, motors of any kind were rare and the customer had little or no experience, he was really on his own; no garages or filling stations every few miles like today. Consequently the catalogue was not only a selling tool but had perforce to be an instruction book, workshop manual, spare parts list and 'How to Ride' tutor all rolled into one. In the 1906 catalogue for example there is a whole page headed 'HOW TO LEARN' which, under seven headings, tells you how to start the engine of your new motorcycle. This is a complicated process where the positions of the tankside-mounted levers all appear to be critical. Having mastered this with the machine on its stand, paragraph 8 tells us

'When sufficiently practised in the management of the levers etc. dismount, wheel machine slightly forward until both wheels are on the ground, raise stand and tightly clamp to guard. Wheel to a quiet road, mount and dismount by pedal; belt may be removed if desired to facilitate this by pulling away from machine (on stand), so as to make it pass outside edge of large pulley, and turning rear wheel slowly forward. Unhook and remove. Mounting etc. mastered, replace belt, securely fasten up stand, slightly flood carburettor, hold up left handle bar lever whilst mounting, pedal and start as on stand, pulling up left handle bar lever directly the sensation of 'going too fast' is experienced, and adhering to previous instructions, particularly those in paragraph 7.'

So we set off on our first ride and we are, lower down on the page, exhorted to 'Keep to the left' and overtake on the right with exception of tramcars, which should 'always be passed inside ie between rails and kerb on the left or near side'. Very valuable advice but no mention, surprisingly, of the danger to motorcyclists of the tram rails, which have caused many riders to dismount violently, including the author.

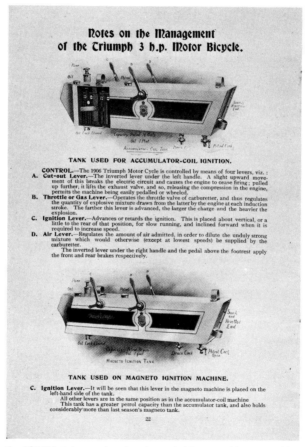

A page from the 1906 Catalogue showing the tankside control levers and how to use them.

Also in the 1906 catalogue under the heading 'Spare Parts and Sundries' we find the following useful advice:-

'We strongly recommend every motorcyclist never to be without the necessary spare parts of which we give particulars and prices below. The valves should be ground into their respective seats, and all other parts similarly tried in place.

		Price	
		s.	d.
Two sparking plugs and washers, best Triumph	ea	5	0
One 15 ah accumulator	"	15	0
One spare valve, spring and cotter	"	5	6
One cam for contact breaker	"	1	6
One pair of spiral springs for contact breaker	pr		6
One platinum pointed screw for contact breaker	ea	2	3
One contact piece with platinum point for con. bkr	"	2	9
One foot of belting	"	1	9
One belt hook (Simplex)	"	1	6
One piston ring	"	1	6
One four-volt lamp, with lens and long cord	"	4	6

This lamp can be used:

A In place of voltmeter. A well charged accumulator will cause filament to glow with a *white* light; if partly down, only a red glow will be obtainable.

B As an inspection lamp at night, more especially when a leak of petrol is suspected.

C As an emergency headlight, tied to head of machine and connected to spare accumulator.

Riding in those far off days was not a simple matter and you had to get things right. It says much for the unquenchable enthusiasm of our forebears that they persevered so that we, today, can press a button and take off without a second thought.

However, in 1908 a big step forward was made when Triumph moved the controls from the tank side to the handlebars, a feature which we take for granted, but it was not always so. We quote,

'One of the many improvements in our 1908 machine is the new Triumph carburetter with handle-bar control. It is a luxury which has only to be tried to be appreciated .....'

Catalogues in the early days always included testimonials from satisfied customers (not only in the early days, come to think of it, I have used them myself on more than one occasion) and today these make quaint reading, like that from Mr J.T. Schwain writing from Cambridge in 1905 – *Dear Sirs, I find her very satisfactory, as she is very comfortable, fast and yet can be ridden slowly in traffic"* or the Rev. B.H. Davies writing in 1907 from Northampton *...again as I ride chiefly on Saturdays, it would be a serious matter for me if I failed to return in time for my Sunday duties. With any other make it would be anxious work to be one hundred miles from my church at 4 pm on Saturday. Riding other makes I keep close to the railway lines as a precaution, and carry a timetable.* The Rev. B.H. Davies was of course the famed contributor "Ixion" of 'The Motor Cycle'.

Triumph has always been a great exporting company and in the 1911 catalogue there are no less than seven testimonials from New Zealand and others from Australia, Ceylon, Burma, Newfoundland and the Federated Malay States. That from Burma testifies to Triumph power.

Bhamo, Upper Burma May 7th 1910. Dear Sirs, I purchased one of your motor bicycles in August last year. From that time until the middle of January last, I used it at home for sidecar work, and sometimes having as much as twenty-eight stones up. I brought the bicycle out with me in January and have used it in Rangoon and this station. I have never,

*since I bought the machine, been stopped on the road by any mechanical or other trouble
....T.S. Blackwell.*

I wonder, did he have a particularly robust wife or was he a scrap metal merchant?

An interesting sidelight to these testimonials is that several of them are from big companies like Massey-Harris and the International Harvester Co of America stating their satisfaction with the Triumph fleets used by their travellers. It seems that the Trusty Triumph was the forerunner of the company car.

In the 32 pages of the 1908 catalogue only two pages are used to describe the machine, its specification and price (£48). Eight pages deal with 'Construction Details'. The Simms-Bosch magneto has four pages, lubrication two pages; testimonials with pictures, four pages; parts list for the magneto three pages; other parts and accessories with prices, two pages (cylinder only, £2). The catalogue was the rider's bible, it told him everything he wanted to know about riding and caring for his motorcycle, what parts he might need and how much they would cost him.

Chapter Three

The Trusty Triumph on active service

I cannot think of a better title for this chapter than the above, which is taken from a booklet of the same name issued by the company during the Great War. The front cover is reproduced here, also the classic drawing done by H. Thomas in 1914 with the story which appeared under it in *Motor Cycling*. The booklet comprises a series of 'Letters from the Front' from riders on active service in all parts of the world. We quote two of these:

Lieut. Takeda, Aviation Corps, Japanese Army. At the outer walls Tsingtau. "...every day I am having pleasant flights over Tsingtau for overhead scouting and bomb throwing. The Triumph motor velo attached to the Aviation Corps has proved its efficiency... over frightfully bad roads, and even when running through river beds where the wheels sink in, the old arms "sto-ting sto-ting" as steadily as ever. When Tsingtau falls I hope to be the first man in on the Triumph".

Pte. E.W. Spencer, Motor Cycle Corps, writes: "Often our only light on our way to the trenches has been the vivid gun flashes, but in full liberty she (this Triumph) has picked her precious path by dodging shell holes, live wires, tubes, gleaming bayonets, and even through showers of whizzing bullets themselves."

"Sto-ting sto-ting" does not sound much like an old Triumph to me but as the letter was written in Japanese characters, maybe the translation is a little doubtful. Private Spencer certainly has a fine turn of phrase.

The cover of the booklet produced by Triumph to commemorate the service of their motorcycles in the Great War.

A dramatic drawing by H.Thomas which appeared in **Motor Cycling** *in November 1914 and was subsequently reproduced in the Triumph booklet. The caption under it read:-*

THE TRUSTY TRIUMPH IN ACTION

Despatch riders have already won admiration from all branches of the Army, and the account of a deed of real heroism performed recently by a Motor Cyclist, will be universally applauded. It was of urgent importance that a message should be carried from the British to the French lines. This could only be done by crossing land that was being swept of rifle and shell fire from the German positions. A motorcyclist made the attempt but was brought down by a bullet. In a moment two more volunteered but both met with the same fate as the first. A fourth made the desperate attempt and crouching over the handlebars' he drove the machine 'all-out' and succeeded in crossing the danger zone. The Commander of the French troops was so pleased with the exploit that he removed the decoration of the Legion of Honour from his own uniform and conferred it upon the brave motorcyclist.

It was in 1914 that Siegfried Bettmann, who was then Mayor of Coventry, received a phone call one Sunday morning from a Capt C.V. Holbrook of the War Office, who asked him if he could get 100 motorcycles packed for immediate despatch to France. This was done and a friendly relationship developed between the two men. Holbrook became the War Office's director of mechanical transport and was responsible for ordering 30,000 Model 'H' Triumphs during the war. In 1919, Colonel Holbrook, as he had become then, was invited to join the board of Triumph. He developed the car side strongly and it was his proposal that motorcycle manufacture should finish in 1935, which led to Sangster's purchase of the motorcycle side. As Colonel Sir Claude Vernon Holbrook, he was at various times Deputy Lieutenant of Warwickshire, a magistrate and a county councillor. He died in 1979 at the age of 93.

A car, a car, was IT [?] by Team weil, frozen up, and hearned up to the heavy driving
studies and to calla dea s of he Great War.

The three-speed hub gear, another transmission alternative available around the 1914 period.

Believed to have been taken in the Middle East during the Great War, this shot shows a railway platelayers trolley powered by a Triumph $3\frac{1}{2}$ hp motorcycle engine. By the way the men are pushing it looks as if a little more power would be welcome.

The machines which performed so staunchly under apalling conditions were, initially, the $3\frac{1}{2}$ hp with free engine or three-speed hub, but these were soon replaced by the new 4 hp (550 cc) model 'H' which boasted a separate Sturmey Archer 3-speed gearbox controlled by a long lever mounted directly on the box. How the belt drive continued to operate in the glutinous Flanders mud is one of the big mysteries — but obviously it did.

Chapter Four

The Priory Street Works

After the war, Triumph continued its model range and the most notable improvement was the adoption of all-chain drive on the new 4 hp Model SD which also boasted the first Triumph-made gearbox. The 4 valve 'Ricardo' model was also introduced at this time but a real bomb-shell was dropped into the motorcycle market for the 1925 season when Triumph announced what they called 'a 4.94 hp machine of Triumph quality and manufacture throughout and incorporating every modern feature of design' for the incredibly low price of £42.17.6 (or £42.75). It was the famous (or infamous) Model 'P'. It did have a few teething troubles concerned with the front brake, the big end and the clutch, but these could not be cured until the first batch of 20,000 had been built. However, the MK 2 when it came out had been 'sorted', and it gradually overcame the poor reputation of its predecessors. Demand was high at this price, as might be expected, and the mighty Priory Street Works really got into top gear with production figures sometimes topping 1000 per week. A booklet produced at the time takes the reader for a guided tour of the works and points out with justifiable pride the efficiency, speed and high quality of the manufacturing processes. The area of the works totalled 500,000 sq ft and 3000 people were employed in it, in fact I believe that it was the biggest factory in Coventry at the time. It stretched right across the area now occupied by the magnificent Coventry swimming pool and the new Cathedral. With 9000 different motorcycle parts, the stock totalled nine million and it was held in 10,000 bins. Yes, 'the Triumph' was a mighty operation in the twenties because it included bicycles and cars as well, but these do not concern us here.

Sensation of the 1925 Season — the Model P Vincent H.R.D. for 1925 shown here in the standard.

The 1924 Model LS, an advanced little 350 with unit-construction gearbox, outside flywheel on the offside and an overhung crank and big end assembly.

The great Priory Street Works from the air, heavily retouched we suspect, but giving a good idea of the size of the place in 1924.

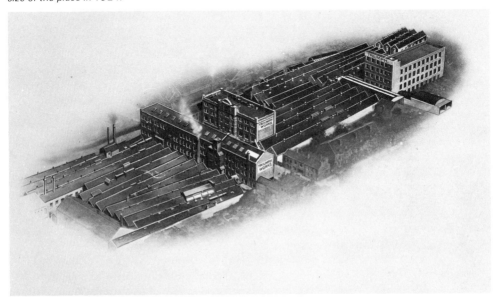

Final Assembly No 2 Shop. Note the separate benches; the assembly track was yet to come. The bikes are the 350 Model LS.

A corner of the Frame Erecting Shop.

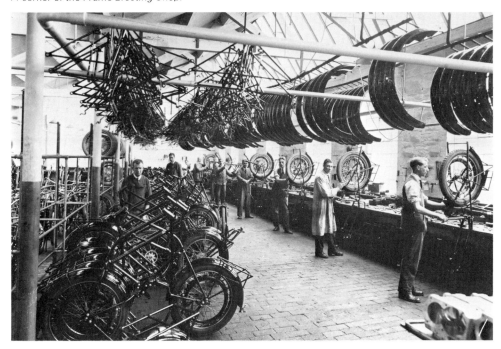

The Wheel Building Shop. Note the 'gaffer' in the center.

The Experimental Department. Odd that there are no motorcycles to be seen anywhere.

Main Machine Shop, Capstan Section. A truly vast area all covered with machines driven by whirling belts.

The Plating Shop. Before the days of chrome.

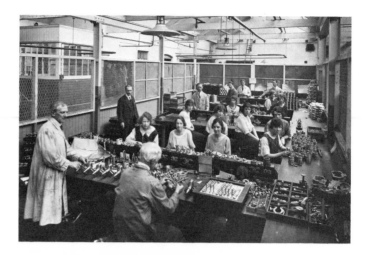

Looking at the photographs of the Works, the first thing a modern observer notices are the masses of belts and pulleys driving the machine tools. A lot of these later found their way into the new Meriden factory after WW2 and were in use there for many years in my time. Another interesting feature one notices looking at these old pictures is that you can nearly always pick out the 'gaffer' of the department. He is the one in the smart suit, usually with a watch chain on his waistcoat, and sometimes he sports a wing collar and bow tie. Very dignified, he stands by himself in the background, but where the camera was sure to catch him. He was indeed a powerful man who could hire and fire as he thought fit, certainly not a man to cross.

One other interesting point concerns the final assembly process. There was no 'track' such as we know today, each motorcycle had its own bench and was assembled virtually complete in one spot. At Meriden, in the late sixties, we sometimes exceeded 1000 machines a week but it was a struggle, even with reasonably current equipment. Of course the modern machine is vastly more complex than the simple old sidevalver but we had only half the number of workers compared with Priory Street forty years before, so we did not do too badly in comparison.

Chapter Five

A transition period

The period between 1932 and 1935 was of immense significance in the Triumph story and what happened in these years enabled the Triumph Engineering Co Ltd, which took over from the old company in 1936, to get off to a good, quick start.

Designer Val Page, a very talented and meticulous motorcycle engineer, joined Triumph from Ariel in 1932, when the company was not in a very happy state. Most of the engineering emphasis was on the cars but there was a motorcycle section in the drawing office and this was in the charge of A.A. Sykes, who had taken over the reorganisation after the slump of 1930. He had produced a commendable single cylinder twin port 500 with sloping cylinder known as the 'Silent Scout'. Commercially it was the Triumph answer to the BSA 'Sloper', which was setting the trend at the time. Most manufacturers had adopted sloping cylinders to counter the BSA challenge, but did it by the simple expedient of pushing the cylinder of their existing upright engine into a slope roughly parallel with the front down tube. Triumph did the job on the drawing board however and made the cylinder fins run parallel to the ground. At least it looked as if the designer had intended the cylinder to slope in the first place, which was more than most of the others did. This model was used by the Coventry police in their 'Flying Squad'. Sykes also produced the ultra-lightweight X model with a 150cc ohv engine, gear primary drive and a unique loop frame. On the experimental side there were a number of projects destined to be abandoned with the arrival of Val Page. One was an hydraulically operated valve mechanism on a side-valve engine. There was also a complete 350cc ohc engine which resembled that of an early KSS Velocette. Also a pressed steel frame on the lines of the Coventry Eagle 'Silent Superb'. But the wider profit margin and the greater commercial prospects of car manufacture had turned the management's interest away from motorcycles which, by 1932, were in urgent need of a shot in the arm. This was provided by Val Page, who was allowed to set up an autonomous motorcycle design team which quickly set about producing a complete new range of motorcycles which owed nothing to its predecessors. These were based throughout on a thorough knowledge of the product, sound engineering principles and a wide experience of value engineering gained during the difficult days at Ariel. Page smartly sidestepped the existing confusion of unit specification and punch card control, commenting 'We'll first make some good motorcycles, then we'll tackle the system'. Val Page's design schemes were a revelation in the Triumph Drawing Office. They were a complete encyclopedia of information in definite dimensions, materials and where necessary, methods. Drawn meticulously accurately in the essential particulars, freehand where unimportant, they saved hours of interpretation time in the detail office. This fabulous effort of rework on the 1934/5 and finally 1936 ranges was cementing the firm foundation on which Edward Turner was subsequently to built.

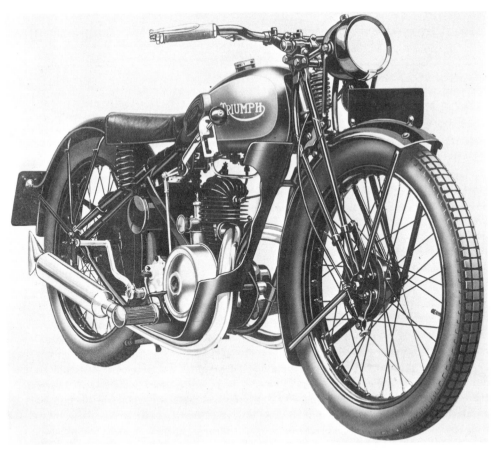

The 150cc Villiers engine was a very popular unit in the early thirties, when many manufacturers offered it in a low price model – even Triumph, who had not used a proprietary engine since before 1905. This was it, the XV/1.

This is Mr. Sykes' X05/5 which seems to bear a close resemblance to the XV/1 apart from the 150cc ohv engine with horizontal fins like its bigger brothers.

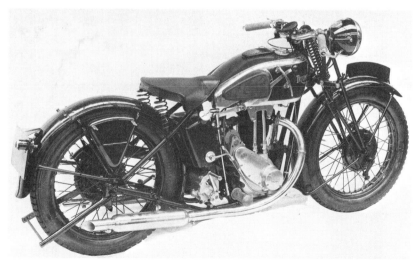

The sure touch of Val Page here. The 250cc 2/1, which later became Edward Turner's Tiger 70, after a little cosmetic treatment.

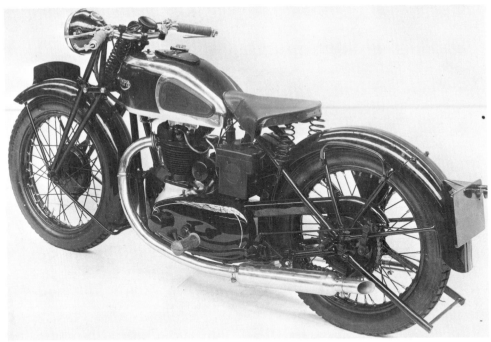

The 3/2, which with a wave of the Turner magic wand turned into the Tiger 80.

Finally Page's 500cc 5/5, which became the Tiger 90. Incredible how a bike can lose weight with a touch of colour and a change of shape.

Page's big twin, the 650cc 6/1. A good, sound, solid motorcycle designed primarily to tow sidecars, which it did very well. Turner discarded it.

Internals of the 6/1. Note the single rear-mounted camshaft and its gear drive extended to the Magdyno. The primary drive was by helical gears.

41

Harry Perrey, competition rider and stunt man extraordinary, poses on a 6/1 sidecar. He won the Maudes Trophy in 1933, with a 500 mile ride in less than 500 minutes, on a 6/1 outfit, with a team of four riders.

Page's new models comprised three 250cc ohv's, one 350cc side-valve, two 350cc ohv's, two 550cc side-valves, four 500cc ohv's and a 650cc ohv twin. There was a high degree of standardisation throughout the range and many major components were shared. The Mk 5 model was the top of the range in each class, if we ignore the 5/10 Mk 10, which was virtually a racer, one 500 (5/5) one 350 (3/2) and one 250 (initially the L2/1) formed the basis of the revamped range in 1936 after Edward Turner had taken over.

In view of the success of Edward Turner's twin it is worth recording some details of Page's 6/1 650cc vertical twin. This machine was not an outstanding success commercially. It was a very sound design with pushrod operated overhead valves worked from a rear mounted camshaft on similar lines to later BSA and Norton twins. It had gear primary drive and a 4-speed gearbox in unit with the engine. It was a heavy machine and its main purpose appeared to be for sidecar work, which it handled very competently. The Turner twin bore no resemblance to the 6/1 in any way. There was yet another Triumph vertical twin which appeared briefly in experimental form in 1913. This was a 600cc side-valve with exhaust valves at the front of the block and inlets at the rear. It also had a horizontally split crankcase on the lines of a car engine. Nothing more was heard of it so one must presume that it became yet another casualty of the Great War.

In spite of this fabulous personal performance by Val Page, the Triumph company was still in serious financial difficulty. The bank had appointed a Receiver in the person of a Mr Graham, to look after its interests, and by January 1936 the news that motorcycle manufacture was to be discontinued reached the ears of Jack Sangster, who sought an interview with Mr. Graham. This proved difficult and the story has often been told that hearing Graham was going to London by train the following morning, Sangster met him at New Street station in Birmingham with a London ticket in his pocket. By the time the train had steamed into Euston, they had agreed the broad terms of purchase. As a result of this quick intervention, production continued in Coventry without any disruption. However, many key people, including Val Page, had left. Page had gone to BSA. In his place the old company had taken on Frank Anstey from Rudge but he had hardly settled in when the upheaval came and, with every good reason to feel bitter, he moved to Ariel as Edward Turner left to come to Triumph — it was a real musical chairs. Jack Sangster had negotiated a very smooth takeover of the motorcycle side and it continued to operate in that part of the old factory which extended from Dale Street to Cox Street. The cars, in the meantime, had moved to the Dennis factory in Holbrooks Lane, which in the Great War had been the White and Poppe munitions factory.

The stage was now set for the Turner revolution.

Chapter Six

An Edwardian start

I have referred briefly in the introduction to Edward Turner who was one of the three giant personalities (Bettmann and Sangster were the other two) on whom the fortunes of Triumph depended for more than eighty years, so at this point we will look at Edward Turner's early life and background, how he became involved with motorcycles and his achievements which finally led him to Triumph.

AN EDWARDIAN START

Edward Turner was born in London on 24th January 1901. The choice of the name was an obvious one as he was born a few hours after the passing of Queen Victoria and thus became the first true Edwardian in the family of seven, having three sisters and three brothers. His father ran a light engineering business, manufacturing a wide range of products for the tradesmen of the day. This engineering environment gave him a close acquaintance with metal, its manipulation and its uses and perhaps the know-how that in later years provided the confidence and sometimes the audacity to make metal work so hard.

His maternal grandparents were engaged in the coachbuilding trade in London, his grandmother in fact being a member of the Hillman family, which later brought fame to Coventry with the Hillman car. At the turn of the century the horse was still the main motive power for urban transport and Edward Turner often spoke of the smell of the streets being his most vivid recollection of London as a boy. Lit by gas lamps and jam-packed with horse drawn coaches, carriages, wagons and hansoms, on a warm summer night the atmosphere could be overpowering. Wandering in and out of the coachbuilding shops young Edward was entranced by an enormous drawing, full scale, of a coach body which occupied an entire wall of the factory building. The graceful curves of its lines fascinated him as did the enormous 'C' springs on which its body was suspended. Maybe it was here that the ideas for the graceful shapes of many Triumph components originated. Things like the nacelle headlamp, the famous bulbous tank and even the humble front number plate which, in 1946, was quite a thing of beauty. In later years he undoubtedly had a good eye for shape and although his creations did suffer to some degree from the use of compasses and French curves, he was the first to recognise an improvement and would usually accept a better line, provided the changes were made in his own office.

A youthful Edward Turner at his desk after the Ariel take-over by Jack Sangster in 1932.

The family engineering business undoubtedly influenced his life-long interest in creative engineering or, as he would describe it, 'To make a blade of grass grow where none has grown before'. At an early age the schoolboy was suggesting methods of improving and modernising manufacture in his father's firm. He used to tell the story of how Turner Senior allowed him to demonstrate a method of low voltage butt welding to replace the traditional blacksmith's hearth and anvil. The scheme worked perfectly but unfortunately every time it was switched on the strain was too much for the primitive electrical supply system of the day and Peckham was plunged into darkness!

He was still at school when the Great War broke out and one by one all his friends and acquaintances were called up or had joined up. Although he was too young to go himself, by the time he was sixteen he had made up his mind, without discussing the matter with his parents, to get into uniform. He gave a false age and joined the Marconi School, where he trained as a wireless operator. Shortly after his seventeenth birthday he was at sea on an armed merchantman. This was a pretty devastating experience for a lad his age straight from school and exposed to the brutalities and coarseness of life at sea in the Merchant Navy. He survived, however, a sadder and wiser man no doubt, and it is curious to record that even the horrors of war did not stifle the love of the sea, which was to come out later in his life when he was able to indulge this love through the purchase and operation of a series of very fine yachts which bore him and his family on many lengthy cruises to the Mediterranean and elsewhere.

Turner with what we think must be an early Ariel Square Four prototype, the chain drive ohc 500. Note the hand gear change.

His brother raced a Harley at Brooklands, this may well be it but the mudguards and carrier contradict the shape of the handlebars!

After the war he made a brief but unsuccessful excursion into the theatre, where he fancied his prospects as a baritone singer, and it was probably about this time that he first began to take an interest in motorcycles, like many young men of his age. His elder brother was the proud owner of a very fast Harley-Davidson and Edward was a frequent visitor to the famous Brooklands race track near Weybridge. Here he would hurl the Harley round the concrete saucer with great aplomb and he made quite a name for himself. The motorcycle interest grew until he finally decided to invest his savings and what was left of his war gratuity in a motorcycle shop at Peckham. This was a typical corner shop of the period and here he operated what would be called today a 'franchise' for Velocettes. In addition, he dealt in and repaired secondhand motorcycles, plus of course the usual accessory trade. The immediate post-war years saw a mushroom growth in the motorcycle industry and the number of different manufacturers was legion. In common with these, Edward Turner had ideas of his own and decided to design and produce a motorcycle in his own workshop, starting from scratch. This was a 350 cc ohc single. Having produced the detail drawings himself, he employed the services of a local pattern maker, and then went on to machine the components on his own lathe, milling machine and bench driller. He even produced his own cutting tools, hardened and ground from ordinary carbon steel, which he found retained its edge long enough at any rate to machine one set. Many years later, when he became Managing Director of Triumph, he caused a major sensation which resounded through the works when he asked the expert turner to move over whilst he himself machined the exact form of a fillet he required. This gained for him a standard of prestige and respect previously unheard of on the shop floor.

A versatile lad, young Edward. Here he is on an ABC twin, with a background that looks like Hyde Park.

Difficult to believe that the man famous for his good looking motorcycles designed this horror. It is a 350 ohc single.

This one has the Turner touch though. It may well be the one he took to Birmingham with him, when joining the Ariel company.

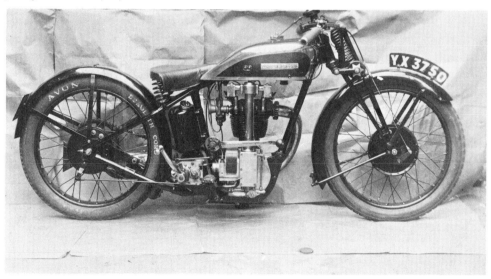

We have two photographs here of ohc Turner machines; one is a rather primitive affair but the other looks highly professional. But there is another 350 ohc engine which Edward Turner designed and which does not appear to have any similarity with those in the photographs. This was described in *The Motor Cycle* dated 16th April 1925 and the drawings show a very interesting design in which the camshaft mounting is cast integrally with one half of the

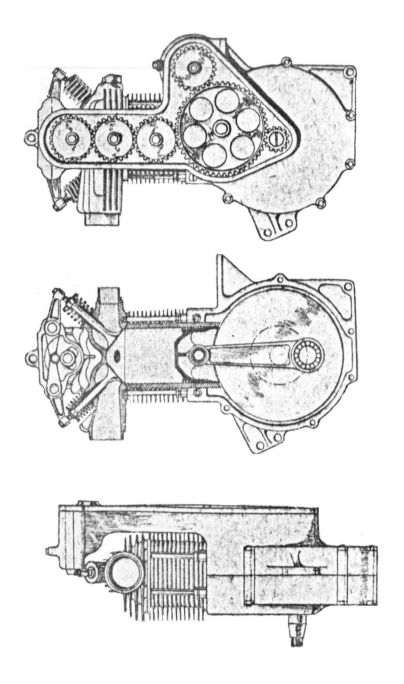

Another Turner engine, this one on paper from **The Motor Cycle** *dated April 16th 1925.*

crankcase. It also forms the casing for the camshaft drive gears. The barrel is sunk deeply into the crankcase and four holding down bolts secure the whole cylinder assembly to the crankcase. Whether the engine was ever made, history does not relate.

With the completion of his 350 cc ohc, Turner was on the look out for someone to make it commercially. He decided to head for the Midlands where all the motorcycle action of the time took place, and here he met John Young Sangster, then boss of Ariel. This meeting was historic, although it is doubtful if either man realised it at the time. Nevertheless it was the start of a very profitable partnership in which both prospered, probably beyond their wildest dreams, in the course of the next forty years. The Sangster family had been involved with the Ariel concern for many years. Known at one time as Components Ltd., it was run by Charles Sangster, J.Y.'s father. 'Mr Jack', as he was called, was Managing Director and in the Ariel Company as Chief Designer was Val Page, one of the finest designers the industry has ever had. When Edward Turner arrived on the scene with his home brewed 350, he was appointed Chief Development Engineer alongside Val Page. His 350 gave him an entry into the industry but it never progressed beyond the prototype stage. He soon became involved in the onward development of the current Ariel range. By the end of the decade the country was heading for a major recession and the Ariel company for bankruptcy. Nevertheless E.T. was fully occupied by now designing and developing his first 'Square Four' power unit. This comprised an incredibly compact arrangement of two 180° crankshafts geared together with solid eye roller bearing big ends assembled on to overhung journals and using light, stiff conventional forged steel connecting rods and light alloy pistons to provide a very good balance arrangement. This first engine was of 500 cc and had a unit 4-speed gearbox in prototype form. The whole

The sign in the first floor window reads 'Turner Equipment Company', that over the shop door 'Chepstow Motors'. In the window can be seen a KSS Velocette. This was Edward Turner's motorcycle shop in Peckham Road, London.

machine was incredibly light and had a tremendous performance for its day. The valve gear was operated by a chain driven, overhead camshaft, working the parallel valves through rockers and driving a distributor on one end. It was unfortunate that the problems facing the company precluded them from going ahead with this machine in the lightweight prototype form. There was no money available for brand new designs off the drawing board. The engine, however, was so promising that it was put into the chassis of the standard 500 cc ohv single cylinder Ariel, with separate gearbox, and this is how it first reached the market place in 1931. The famous 'Square Four' Ariel continued in the Ariel range from 1932 right through to 1952 but over the years it was redesigned from time to time, first into a pushrod 600 cc and then jumped up to 1000 cc, which was the ultimate, and in this form it made a world-wide name for itself as a fantastically smooth, quiet tourer with tremendous acceleration. Today it is a much sought-after vintage model.

Earlier in the book we referred to the Triumph Company being in low water in 1932 and bringing in Val Page as Chief Designer. He came, of course, from Ariel, where he left Edward Turner sitting in the Chief Designer's chair. From here E.T. directed the design fortunes of the company to some tune and his Red Hunter range restored the Ariel fortunes in no uncertain manner. These handsome singles proved themselves as good as they looked. They were fast, rugged and reliable. They did well in competition, in trials, scrambles and even at Brooklands they proved their worth. Edward Turner's treatment of them was to be paralleled later when he moved over to Triumph. He took an existing design and, by deft styling and brilliant engineering 'streamlining', he turned what was a run of the mill motorcycle into a highly desirable property. Not only that but his cost cutting and metal paring enabled the product to earn a handsome profit, which is what business is all about.

Chapter Seven

The new company sets to work

The name adopted by the new company was the Triumph Engineering Co. Ltd. Now this was not a new name, having been first registered by the old company on 23rd April 1906, with a capital of £100. Why this was done history does not relate but on 25th February 1936 the capital was increased to £21,000. It is of interest to note that the first company name using Triumph was registered in 1897 as the 'New Triumph Cycle Co. Ltd.' and later in 1897 the 'New' was dropped. In December 1930, when cars began to play a bigger part in the company's operations, the 'Cycle' was dropped too and the name became 'Triumph Company Limited'. In connection with this latter company the Receiver announced in October 1939 that all assets had been disposed of and no funds were available for winding up the company. However, in 1936 the young Triumph Engineering Co. Ltd. was all set to go places and announced the name of its first Chairman, Mr. Stanley Evershed of Evershed & Tomkinson, solicitors. This was obviously a temporary arrangement and on 20th July he was replaced by none other than the original founder of the company, Siegfried Bettmann. This was an astute move to add respectability to the new organisation and to encourage suppliers to keep supplying after a period in which they had become understandably cautious. Mr Bettmann was in the Chair at the Inaugural Luncheon of the new company held at the King's Head Hotel Coventry on 27th January 1936, to which a large number of Triumph dealers and suppliers were invited. However Bettmann's term of office did not last long, to quote his own words — 'Mr Sangster called on me and asked me to be Chairman of the Company to which was given the name of Triumph Engineering Co. Ltd. I agreed to do so, but for some reason into which it is not necessary to go further, but which was of the most friendly character, I (soon) retired from the Chairmanship and this ended my active commercial life'.

Author's Note. 'I had the privilege of meeting Mr Bettmann at Meriden shortly after the war. He was a short gnome-like man with a very heavy German accent. This was remarkable in view of the fact that he had lived in England for more than sixty years at that time.

With Siegfried Bettmann finally retired, Jack Sangster took his place as company Chairman, with Edward Turner as Managing Director and Chief Designer. It fact it became abundantly clear in no time at all that as MD he was not only Chief Designer but Chief Sales Executive, Chief Buyer, Chief Engineer, Chief Stylist – in short Great White Chief, full stop.

Sangster and Turner's first job on acquiring the company was to go right through the works and conduct a machine-by-machine inspection of the available equipment and decide what they were going to keep and what they were going to dispose of. It must be borne in mind that additional expenditure was out of the question for the time being and onward manufacturing plans were obviously going to be geared very largely to existing plant.

The Coventry Corporation had in fact already acquired the Triumph premises on both sides of Priory Street for re-development purposes but, thanks to Hitler's bombers which laid the whole area flat in 1940, this work never started and it was not until long after the war that the new and controversial Coventry Cathedral rose close to the side of the old works. However, we are getting ahead of ourselves here and back in 1936 the Triumph Engineering Co. Ltd. started operations in the old factory but using only the ground, first and second floors. The two floors above this were used as an overflow space for spares, repairs and a museum corner. It was a well equipped and laid out works with a good machine shop and tool room, brazing, welding, plating and polishing departments and an up-to-date conveyor in the enamelling shop manned by expert sprayers and liners. The material control and stores operation worked on a somewhat rule-of-thumb system and relied on good memories but it worked well for all that. The main assembly track was run by people with years of motorcycle experience behind them, backed up by engine, gearbox and wheel building sections and a very efficient little inspection department. All the other usual factory services were on tap – works engineers, millwrights, transport, canteen and surgery, etc. Radiating out from this hub was the vast worldwide dealer network controlled by the sales organisation. In short, Sangster and Turner had inherited a going concern but it was not going very well. Nevertheless it developed from this point into one of the most commercially successful and profitable small companies of any type ever to operate in this country. Not that any of the employees had any idea of the successful future that stretched ahead. Most of them were only too glad still to have jobs and many of these were at reduced wages. But all the components necessary for a successful business were present and it needed only a good spark to set it off. This was provided by Edward Turner in no uncertain manner. He quickly ordered an area in the assembly shop to be partitioned off, with his own office occupying one corner, the Drawing Office on his left approached through one door and the General Office forward of him, approached through the other door, from which position he could survey the entire area. So work started. There was what can only be described as a skeleton staff in the General Office and four young and enthusiastic draughtsmen as the nucleus of a design team. These were headed by Bert Hopwood, who had followed his old boss from Ariel. Turner looked at the existing range of Triumph models with a very clear plan of action. It was essential to reduce immediately the multiplicity of component parts, simplify and rationalise manufacture and eliminate unprofitable projects. Costs must be cut, but out of all this must come a range of impact-making products in the shortest possible time. A tall order but one which could be and was done. First, one model from each of the three capacity classes was taken and with a minimum of mechanical change at first, was given a face lift with a brand new livery, a lot of showroom glitter and, perhaps most important of all a swash-buckling sporty name. Thus were born the Triumph 'Tigers'. Page's 500 cc 5/5 became the 'Tiger 90', the 3/2 350 cc became the 'Tiger 80' and the L2/1 250 cc the 'Tiger

Two of the greatest designers the motorcycle industry in the United Kingdom has known. Val Page and Edward Turner deep in discussion.

70'. This latter only ran for one season and was replaced by the 2/1 model, which had many parts common with the 350 cc. The L2/1 was, in fact, one of the best 250's ever produced in this country but it was expensive to make and unprofitable. It had a unique integrally forged flywheel and mainshaft set-up which was quite the best of its kind, a fact that was quickly recognised by competition riders everywhere who proceeded to extract phenomenal performances from the engine. But it had to go. Retailing at £38, Turner claimed that the company was giving away a fiver in the toolbox of every one.

It is of interest to see what was done to these motorcycles to convert them almost overnight from also-rans to world beaters. It is a process that today in industry is accepted as commonplace and obvious — styling. In those days the appearance of the product was usually something which just happened when the engineers had finished their work. If it looked right, so much the better, if it did not, the public would soon find out that it was well engineered and buy it — so they thought. Proportions, shape, colour, sparkle make the product look good in the showroom, and today the stylists work side by side right through the project, adding a touch here, a curve there. This saves cost as re-design is expensive. So, what did Turner do to Page's motorcycles? Completely new bulbous chrome-plated petrol tanks finished in silver sheen with dark blue lining and with a most attractive rubber moulded knee grip. A new handlebar, abandoning for all time the traditional Triumph inverted clutch and brake levers. These were replaced with adjustably-mounted long TT type levers. Plated wheels and spokes with silver sheen centres lined in blue, 3 inch ribbed front tyres, high level exhaust pipes, a finned exhaust

The 250cc Tiger 70. Initially this was based on the L2/1 but was quickly changed to the 2/1 which had a greater degree of commonality with the other models in Page's range.

The 350cc Tiger 80. Derived from the previous 3/2.

Page's 3/1 side valve in its original form. This too was given the Turner 'treatment' as was its 600cc sister but all side valves were discontinued after the war.

The 250cc L2/1. 'One of the best 250's produced in this country'. Regrettably it was expensive to make and unprofitable so it was dropped by Turner.

The Inaugural Luncheon of the Triumph Engineering Co Ltd held at the Kings Head Hotel Coventry on 27th January 1936. One of the few photographs which include the 'Big Three' of Triumph on the same picture. Edward Turner on the extreme right, Bettmann in the centre of the top table and Sangster just beyond him.

The Inaugural Luncheon, some of the dealers and suppliers who attended. The banner says 'You can always trust the Trusty Triumph'. How right that proved to be.

pipe clip (still used today), a tank top instrument panel, chrome-plated saddle springs, headlamp and fork links. All these external items plus highly polished aluminium timing covers and chaincases spelt instant success in the showroom and sporting motorcyclists clamoured to buy the Tigers– the Triumph Engineering Company had got off to a good start. Similar treatment was given to the other models in the range, both ohv and sv, but the sales emphasis was on the 'Tigers'. Edward Turner's dynamic approach was having a profound effect in all parts of the organisation and particularly in the areas where his day-to-day contacts and interests urged on the various projects which were in the pipe line. Quite apart from the engineering, which was his obvious interest, he kept the sales people on their toes, met and talked to dealers, supervised very closely the production of all advertising and sales literature and watched buying prices with an eagle eye working in fractions of a farthing.

Turner was no mean rider either and as a young man was often reluctant to accept the verdict of the professional testers on anything new. He would hare up the road with the brim of his trilby hat flattened against the crown, too impatient even to wait for trade plates to be fitted. He usually returned with a positive opinion and instructions to proceed forthwith or, on the rare occasion, some comment like 'We'll have another look at it', and so – back to the drawing board. At this time, of course, and for many years after, into the sixties in fact, all machines were road tested prior to delivery. Today the 'Rolling Road' reigns supreme, a device which monitors the performance of all the major functions, lubrication, gearbox, clutch, electrics, brakes, carburation, horsepower etc., all without the motorcycle moving an inch. A full check takes about fifteen to twenty minutes and there is an added bonus, particularly in winter time, that the risk of picking up salt from the roads is entirely eliminated. Months later in California or some other distant spot the salt has had time to play havoc with the plating and paintwork, which meant the bikes had to be stripped and refinished locally at high cost.

Chapter Eight

The Speed Twin

The modern Triumph logo 'cleaned up' by the Drawing Office after the war on Turner's instructions. No departure from this form was permitted but the versions used on things like footrest rubbers were not very accurate.

There are two small but important points of interest in connection with the earliest days of the Turner regime at Triumph and these concern the famous Triumph namestyle and the familiar blue 'house' colour. The namestyle with the large 'T' and the tail of the 'R' sweeping under to join the cross-piece of the 'H' had been used by Triumph in a variety of shapes since the twenties. Turner demanded that 'the shape be unvarying and as readily recognised as the London Underground sign'. It was redrawn in the Drawing Office to a cleaner crisper outline and from that day to this no other has been used and woe betide anyone who 'mucked about' with it. Three versions of the name are illustrated here, pre and post Great War, and the current version. The blue he was aiming for was a traditional Coventry blue, a colour which it is claimed dates back far into the medieval life of the city and was associated with the

This is how it was before the Great War. There were slight variations occasionally but this was the shape they used on catalogue covers.

development of the process of felting wool and its application to the manufacture of hats which, for centuries, had been dyed this traditional colour. 'Triumph Blue' can be seen on exhibition stand carpets, posters, signs, catalogues, stickers, ties etc, but unlike the namestyle it can vary due to the vagaries of printers ink although every effort is made to keep it consistent. The very first application of this blue was the lining on the tank of the original 'Tigers' to complement the silver sheen.

To move on to the vertical twin engine which set the trend for the next forty years, Edward Turner made some notes about this after the war and this is what he said:-

This came from a 1922 catalogue. Oddly enough, in that same year on parts lists and bicycle catalogues, the logo used is virtually identical to the modern one.

The Master and his Masterpiece.

When I was Development Engineer for Ariel I decided to make a Square Four. Mr Page the Chief Designer took a great interest in the work. Having finished the 500cc Square Four I took out the front crankshaft, reversed the throws to give 360 degree crank location on the rear end crankshaft and by dividing the camshaft and retarding it to give the necessary proper cam relation I had what is to all intents and purposes the modern layout of a vertical twin. This was done experimentally to see how a little 250cc twin would work and it worked extremely well. It was very smooth and as Mr Page at the time said 'makes you wonder if you want a four cylinder at all'.

Mr Page later joined Triumph and his impressions of the experimental 250cc twin led him to design a 650cc vertical twin. This was made and sold in relatively small numbers and did not appear to have any wide appeal, although it was an extremely good machine from an engineering point of view. The valve gear layout was the same as that later used by BSA and Norton i.e. a single camshaft at the back with pushrods between the cylinders.

When I took over Triumph in 1936 it was my intention to introduce a vertical 500 twin and in 1938 I offered one to the public known as the 'Speed Twin' which was an entirely new mechanical layout. The principal features of this engine were that it had an inside flywheel supported mid-way between the crank journals by a stiff web. Two camshafts, one on either side of the barrel gave a much more symmetrical layout and enabled more air to pass through the cylinders and over the head. The general proportions of this engine were most eyeable and in performance it was even more remarkable inasmuch that the first prototype was producing nearly 30 hp.

The new engine was of 63mm bore and 80mm stroke. This maintained commonality with the 250cc engine and used existing manufacturing tackle and gauges etc for cylinder bores, pistons, little ends and gudgeon pins. It also utilised existing compression and scraper rings on the pistons, and common gudgeon pins and circlips. The existence of parts 'on the shelf' Turner used to say, decided his bore and stroke in this case.

Jack Wickes, Turner's PA on the design side, said some years later that at this time Turner was the owner of a fairly mellow Riley Nine car, for which he had an unusually high regard. To extract the last ounce of performance out of this to enable him and his wife to get to London and back for an evening out, Turner had the Experimental Department machine 30 thou off the cylinder head, to boost the compression ratio. Wickes at the time could not help noticing the similarity when comparing the cross section of the new Triumph engine with its hemispherical heads, 90 degree valves, short rockers and pushrods and equally disposed fore and aft camshafts with the end view of the gaffer's Riley Nine. But as Turner himself would have said 'There's nothing new under the sun my boy' and there really is no resemblance apart from the broad concept.

So the Speed Twin burst on an unsuspecting public and they liked what they saw – it was a sensational success from the word go. Its performance, its smoothness, its ease of starting and control captivated the motorcyclist of the day brought up on big singles.

Authors note – I was one of these. I bought a 1938 Speed Twin secondhand in the early days of the war and could run rings round a friend of mine who was an ardent Norton fan and who owned a current Model 18. I will admit that the steering at high speed was a little hairy on the Triumph but the acceleration was incredible after a single.

The Speed Twin engine with the dynamo in the front and the magneto at the rear, also the engine shaft shock absorber.

A sectioned Tiger 100 engine, early post-war. This was an Earls Court Show unit; note the glittering finish.

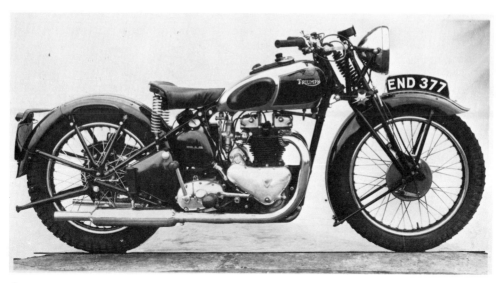

A restored 1938 'six-stud' Speed Twin. The barrel fixings were increased to eight the following year as there had been a few cases of the barrel and crankcase parting company under severe stress.

Nearside view of the same machine; the polished aluminium primary chaincase was an attractive eyecatcher.

The 1939 Tiger 100. A real flyer, this pre-war Tiger. Each one had a certificate of performance supplied to the buyer. The gallon oil tank and 'megaphone' silencers were features.

One other cunning point about the Speed Twin was that it looked like an ordinary two port single so that the prejudices against something different were not aroused. At £74 it was a sure starter and queues almost formed at the dealers shops. Simple, easy and cheap to make, the Triumph vertical twin engine since that time has powered hundreds of thousands of motorcycles and has been in continuous production longer than the Volkswagen. It responds spectacularly to tuning, it has held the world motorcycle speed record and won races everywhere. It started a vertical twin bandwagon on to which almost every other manufacturer in UK and abroad has since jumped, and it enabled Turner to build Triumph Engineering into a company which, at the height of its fame, probably made more profit per pound invested than any similar company before or since.

It also made Turner a rich man and in later years he lived in some style. He was a dominant character whose presence could never be ignored. Churchillian in figure and possessing, like that great man, considerable oratory powers, he commanded respect wherever he went. His staff learned through bitter experience to live with his often violent temper, which usually subsided as quickly as it arose.

Authors Note I worked for him for the best part of twenty years and was very familiar with this side of his character. One thing I will say about him, unlike a lot of big bosses he did not expect his staff to be 'yes men', far from it. You could say what you liked providing it made sense and he would listen. He was also, again unlike many bosses, readily accessible to his staff. If you wanted to see him it was only necessary to check that he was alone then knock on his door and be invited in.

Where the first Speed Twins were built. This is the assembly track at the Priory Street works in 1939.

Packing the 'Tigers' at Priory Street pre-war. The cases to the centre rear are stencilled for Melbourne, Australia.

The Speed Twin came as a rude shock to companies like BSA, Matchless, Royal Enfield and even that impregnable stronghold of the single, Norton. They all reached for their drawing boards but the war intervened before any of them could produce a competitor to the Speed Twin. In 1939 Turner went one better by announcing a super sports version of the Speed Twin called, logically enough, Tiger 100. This was a real flyer and each one was sold with a certificate of performance. At this point the lights went out over Europe and war came. This was to be a traumatic experience for Triumph but it succeeded, like many other factories in Coventry, in rising Phoenix-like from the ashes, as we shall see.

Chapter Nine

World War II leads to Meriden

The outbreak of war in 1939 and the proposed introduction of a new 350 twin virtually coincided, so the twin finished up 'on the shelf' until it was dusted off six years later and put into the post-war programme as the 3T.

Motorcycles for military use were the immediate requirement and the authorities impressed the entire civilian output, including Speed Twins and Tiger 100's, and 1400 machines were despatched in six weeks. Production was then concentrated on the 350 side valve but early in 1940 a French Government contract for 500cc side valve machines was completed. Other production at this time included large quantities of aircraft components, tank track links, steering housings, two-wheeled stretcher carriages and a power driven winch for installation in target towing aircraft utilising the 500cc twin engine. Edward Turner had produced an entirely new military motorcycle, an ultra-light 350 twin with a unit gearbox and for the first time ever, an alternator on the crankshaft to provide current for lighting. This machine had passed its tests so successfully that it was the intention of the Government to standardise it for service use and all manufacturers would have been obliged to make it. The first batch was almost ready for despatch when the Luftwaffe reduced a large part of the Coventry city centre to rubble, including the Triumph factory. That was the sad end of the 3TW. Incredibly, there were no casualties among the Triumph night shift who were on that night.

Rescuing whatever could be rescued, Triumph moved into an old foundry at Warwick, which was rapidly converted into a machine shop and the production of parts for Army machines was commenced. By June 1941, complete machines (the 350 ohv 3HW developed from the Tiger 80 but with rocker boxes cast integrally with the head) were coming off the track once more. The Warwick works, known affectionately as 'The Tin Tabernacle' was on the Grand Union Canal and lunch time siestas on the canal banks came as a new experience to

69

the Triumph workers. The bargees' pub, the 'Cape of Good Hope' was a popular rendezvous at the end of the day.

Meanwhile, a site at Meriden outside the city had been selected for a new factory. Work commenced in July 1941 and by March 1942 some machinery was actually installed and in operation, a timescale which would be difficult to equal in today's conditions. War is a powerful incentive.

Despite the destruction of the Coventry works, Triumph actually produced 49,700 motorcycles during the war period, comfortably in excess of the total made for the Great War (30,000) when there had been no violent interruptions. This, of course, was in addition to the many other products turned out to help the war effort. One of these, a generator set for the RAF, employed the 500cc twin engine as its motive power, and to cut the weight down an alloy head and barrel were designed. These were put to good use after the war on the Grand Prix and Trophy models.

These dramatic pictures, taken by Alec Masters, Triumph Service Manager at the time, show the devastation wrought at the Priory Street works during the Coventry blitz on 14 November 1940.

What was left of the erecting shop with many burnt out motorcycles in the foreground.

Remains of the Sub Assembly Shop and Service Stores. Coventry Cathedral spire can be seen to the left of the Triumph building – it is still there today.

Lower part of the picture is the Electric Transformer House, various offices and stores were in the upper part.

The effect of heat on one of the main girders in the Service Stores.

A scene of utter desolation.

The name lives on, but not much else.

The 'Tin Tabernacle' at Warwick. The offices were housed in here with the 'works' in buildings at the rear. The chapel bell made a good target for airgun firing draughtsmen. The motorcycles, both 350's, one an ohv the other a sidevalve.

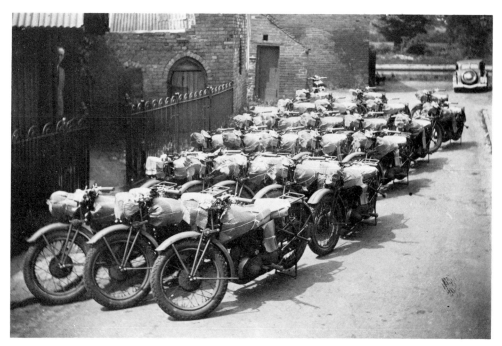

A batch of WD motorcycles awaiting despatch from Warwick.

The Triumph design team at Warwick in 1941. Jack Wickes in front, Horace Watson centre and Bert Hopwood at the back.

Horace Watson and Bert Hopwood ponder a problem at Warwick in 1941.

The Triumph 3HW 350 ohv for the Services. Basically a Tiger 80 but with integrally cast rocker boxes due to the wartime scarcity of aluminium.

An aerial view of the Meriden Works taken after the war but this is how it looked 'as built' in 1942. The vacant areas to the right, left and rear were completely built over in subsequent years, as the business expanded.

*This was the first consignment of motorcycles to be built in the new Meriden factory –
3HW's for the army.*

*Side valves for the girls – but two of them are misguided enough to ride some other make. Despatch
riders from the WRNS.*

The manufacturers drew lots to see who would build the 400,000th British WD motorcycle. Triumph won, of course. Edward Turner can be seen making a point to Jack Welton, Manager of the Sales Department.

The Ground Generator Set built by Triumph for the RAF. It incorporated a 500cc twin engine, fan cooled and using a special alloy head and barrel to save weight.

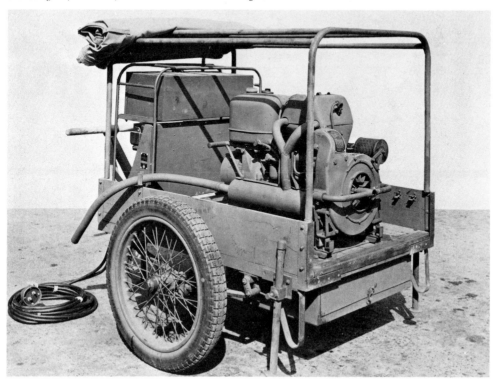

The alloy head and barrel used on the Generator Set and which were later put to good use on the Grand Prix and Trophy models after the war.

Triumph advertising in wartime was nothing if not patriotic.

Chapter Ten

The story changes

Up to here this story has been put together by extractions from private papers and biographies, files, catalogues and from tapes prepared by Jack Wickes. From this point on the author has joined Triumph Engineering Co Ltd as Publicity Manager, so the narrative takes on a more personal angle and now becomes, to some extent 'Triumph from the inside', which was not always as peaceful as it may have looked from the outside.

Before the war I worked for one of the world's leading advertising agencies so had a fair knowledge of my 'trade' but in January 1946, when I joined Triumph as Publicity Manager, I was pretty rusty after six years in the army. I had actually negotiated the Triumph job in 1939 but being a Territorial DR in Signals I was called up even before hostilities commenced, so was unable to move to Coventry. Languishing in the jungles of Burma six years later, with the war obviously drawing to a close, I decided to open negotiations with Triumph again and received a favourable reply asking me to call them then I was demobbed. This I did: I was interviewed at Meriden by Edward Turner and Charles Parker, Company Secretary, and offered a job on the spot which I accepted just as promptly.

Under Edward Turner's dynamic direction the rust fell off very rapidly. Soon I was back in the old business dealing with the press, the printers, the blockmakers, the artists and photographers and all who go to make up the fascinating business of publicity. As it was all tied up with my favourite sport, motorcycling, and my favourite make, Triumph, the outlook appeared idyllic, combining business with pleasure in the biggest possible way. But the boss was a hard man to work for and he knew everything about everything (or nearly so) and demanded perfection, speed of working and the lowest possible cost consistent with high quality. He was very short tempered and would storm and rage if things were not done as he wanted them or at the time that he wanted them. However the storms blew over quickly and if one did produce something he liked, the fact that he made no comment was praise indeed.

My brief was a very wide one. Exhibitions, advertising, publicity (not the same thing), printing, photography, competition admin. functions, taking visitors round the works and buying typewriters. You may well ask the size of the department responsible for all these important areas. It was just myself and a charmingly shy little secretary, Sheila, fresh out of school. Triumph was a very efficiently run outfit with a very small senior staff. There was no empire building and no over-manning — quite the opposite in fact.

For many years the demand for Triumph was so high that strictly speaking, there was no need for any advertising at all, but it was important to keep the name in front of the public and necessary to support the motorcycling journals of the day. Any kind of hard sell was out. It was at this time that we ran a series of cartoon advertisements produced by Alex Oxley, who had made a name for himself in the pages of *Motor Cycling*. These ads were based on the slogan 'It's easy on a Triumph' and portrayed some barely credible feat which it was suggested could be accomplished on a Triumph, complete nonsense of course, but great fun. Some of these are shown here — they caused quite a stir at the time and many chuckles. We had some riotous times thinking up new situations for Oxley to illustrate — even the MD had a go — but most came from the artist himself. So our advertising was very restrained for quite a long time. We were hard put to it sometimes to devise wording which registered Triumph but did not promote too much action on the part of the would-be customer. What a situation for an ad man to find himself in. However there was one area where we could and did let ourselves go. This was in advertising competition successes which the Triumph trials team in the fifties and sixties achieved with some regularity. The trade supported trials were the only ones we were permitted to advertise by agreement in the trade, and the International Six Days was a happy hunting ground for Triumph teamsters. We made the most of it with advertisements and posters galore.

IT'S EASY ON A TRIUMPH

Some of the Oxley series of advertisements which appeared in the motorcycle press in the late forties.

Turner was fully aware of the 'power of the press' and made great efforts to cement friendly relationships with the two journals that were published in his time – *Motor Cycling* edited by Graham Walker and *The Motor Cycle* edited by Arthur Bourne. Both were great characters and I am sure that they had tremendous respect for ET as a leader of the industry. Turner used to refer affectionately to Arthur Bourne as the 'Grand High Lama' of motorcycling and would discuss with him at great lengths his ideas and schemes for future developments.

Edward Turner and Graham Walker, Editor of Motor Cycling. The Speed Twin on the left is a 1938 'six-stud', that on the right a 1959 unit construction 5TA.

Things did not always run smoothly though and road tests were a source of great friction from time to time. Mind you, the road tests of those days were milk and water affairs compared to the analytical treatises which appear today, with all their charts, graphs and technicalities – not to mention their extremely brutal criticisms. This would never have done in the old days. If a bike blew up under road test it was clearly understood that it would be spirited discreetly back to the works for rectification and not a word would be printed. Just occasionally, a mild comment that the speedometer was 10% out at 85 mph, or that the front brake appeared to be susceptible to wet weather, would appear, and this would cause fireworks at Meriden. Turner would deny it flatly to the press and then play hell with experimental for letting a bike go out with these defects.

Later, we had Bob Holliday and Harry Louis as editors and again the friendly relationships continued. They were men whose views were respected and whose advice and help could be relied on for the good of the industry or sport. They could also be trusted absolutely not to break an embargo on a press release or any other confidential information which had been given to them.

Another great character with whom I was more personally involved was Frank Hullett, Advertisement Manager for *The Motor Cycle*. He was a cheery, bluff, noisy man who loved his beer and was good company at all times. He would make strenuous efforts to sell me four-colour covers at what I considered were outrageous prices and we had great fun bargaining, usually over a pint. Then there was journalist Charlie Markham of *Motor Cycling*, one of the true greats of the press world – never a dull moment when Charlie was around; his fund of stories was endless. He turned up one day at Meriden with one of the new Sunbeam S7 twins on road test. This was the 500 with the in-line twin engine, shaft drive and big fat tyres – the tourer de luxe, in fact. Of course we all had to have a gallop on it, which we did in turn, but the great Ernie Nott of Isle of Man fame was a long time coming back and he eventually crawled in to the works with a broken frame. The Sunbeam had succumbed to Ernie's strong right wrist, which put Charlie in something of a state, as he visualised telling this story to our deadly enemies at Small Heath when he took the bike back. This was a challenge to our experimental lads and they soon had the frame welded up and repainted as good as new, much to Charlie's relief. It is significant that shortly after this, BSA decided to rubber mount the Sunbeam engine to alleviate the vibration problems from which it suffered. Poor Charles, he was killed when an artic side swiped him as he was waiting at some traffic lights on a works 350 twin trials bike which I had loaned him to ride in the Press Trial.

The annual catalogue was one of the big jobs of the year – this was our principal selling aid and it had to be out in time for the Earls Court Show in November. Before the war Edward Turner had already established a successful format for a Triumph catalogue in the shape of a 12 page book, 8" x 10" oblong (or 'landscape' to be technically correct). This format was continued after the war and the reason why it was this shape is interesting. Turner always insisted that we used a flat side-on view of the motorcycles in the catalogue as this was the view that the designer saw when designing, so it must be the most attractive view. Oddly enough, it is not possible to see a motorcycle in this position unless you are kneeling on the ground, which is not very often I suppose. So to fit the catalogue round a motorcycle at this angle it just had to be landscape. Up to 1938 the catalogue was restricted to two colours, blue and black; with these it was possible to reproduce the silver, black and blue of the Tigers very accurately. However, the arrival of the Speed Twin in amaranth red complicated matters and although two colours were retained in 1938, after that four colours were used, which enabled a true representation of the colour to be offered.

After the war when I came on the scene, this format was continued. The catalogue took three months to produce, one month for the art work, photography and copywriting, one month for blockmaking, typesetting and proofing and one month for printing. Each of the four colours took a week to print the 200,000 copies we used to have. Today, with modern litho processes, the printing could probably be done in half the time or less. Before the advent of colour photography we used black and white photographs of the bikes which were then converted to colour by retouching artists – and very skilful they were too. This procedure had many advantages. Prototype motorcycles for photography are very hard to come by as, although all the modifications have been designed there are no samples of the parts available months before, when you want them. With black and white work it is a simple matter for the artist to draw in, say, a different silencer on his final colour picture, working from engineering drawings. Also it is possible to improve the look of the bike by painting out all the stray cables and odds and ends which stick out and look untidy (a practice on which Turner insisted). This is not practicable with colour photography.

Shortages in all things were common in post-war years and paper was desperately difficult to get from time to time, particularly the high quality art paper necessary to get good reproduction from the four-colour blocks we used for the illustrations of the bikes. I recall one very bitter episode connected with the paper shortage. We were well on with the preparatory work of the catalogue and the printing order had been placed with our usual printer in Coventry. Very soon we were alerted to the fact that the promised paper was not forthcoming. There were daily phone calls between the department and the printers which got more desperate day by day. At last I had no option but to report the situation to the Managing Director, who reaction was predictable — he blew his top! And continued to blow it daily thereafter, most of his venom being directed at me, as if it were my fault. This was hard to bear and finally one day when he roared that he was not interested in paper, he wanted his catalogues, I had had enough. I pointed out quite politely that it was not possible to have catalogues without paper. I thought he was going to explode and I got to wondering whether there were any jobs going at BSA. However things quietened down and after a further acrimonious session with the owner of the printing works, Edward Turner just had to wait. We got the paper in the end, *and* the catalogues, but it was a rough period while it lasted.

We have always been involved with advertising agents — these are the people who tell you how much money you must spend on advertising to sell the number of bikes you are scheduled to make. As they usually work on a commission basis, their estimates tend to be on the generous side and have to be cut down to the amount allocated by a mean minded board whose first reaction when times get tough is to cut advertising, instead of increasing it. But, by and large, the agents do a good job and I built up an excellent rapport with most of the companies we employed — because they changed from time to time. Usually they were from Birmingham but occasionally someone high up thought we should do better if we went to London, despite the fact that it was 100 miles away. I often felt that the board members made these changes purely for snob reasons; it sounded better in the club if your company was using a prestige outfit from London.

I shall never forget the time when a bunch of ideas men came up from the London agency to familiarise themselves with the Tina Scooter which we were about to launch. This had automatic transmission which really worked very well indeed, when everything was right. As it was a very wet day, the test rides were to take place in one of the big shops at Meriden, which happened to be empty at the time, pending some reorganisation or other. There was plenty of room to ride round in it quite comfortably. We showed these lads how easy the Tina was to ride — start up, open the throttle and away you go, no gears, no clutch, dead easy. All proceeded smoothly until one member of the party climbed on who had never ridden anything other than a push bike before. He set off quite smoothly but we were horrified a minute later when, instead of shutting off as he approached the wall at the far end, he opened the throttle flat. Fortunately he braked at the same time, but being unable to free the engine until the revs had dropped, he finished up in a tangle on the floor. When he had recovered sufficiently to speak, he explained that as the front brake lever pulled towards him to stop he thought that the twist grip should do the same. Logical but disastrous! On the T10 as the later development of the Tina scooter was called, the front brake lever was on the left handlebar, which meant that the rider had only one control to operate with each hand, a very sensible arrangement but one which caused some raised eyebrows among the traditionalists.

Apart from the catalogue, the other big annual job was the Earls Court Show in November. This really put pressure on everyone as it had an inescapable deadline — opening day. For many years after the war, the bikes which appeared on the Triumph stand at the show took months to build. Practically every external part was specially finished and even things like the crankcases were polished and sprayed silver. Sparkplugs were chrome plated and the paintwork was polished to such a high degree that the actual thickness of paint left on was minimal but it looked glorious. I know it was minimal because one year I bought one of the show bikes afterwards and all the paint fell off inside three months. The works took great pride in turning out these 'Show finished' bikes and I never heard any customers complain that the bikes they bought from the dealers shop subsequently were not nearly so shiny. This practice cost the earth to do, of course, and was discontinued later.

Some idea of the beauty of the 'Show Finished' motorcycles can be gained from this photograph of a Thunderbird. Every visible part was specially finished; it cost a lot of money.

The design of the stand took a lot of time and thought and Edward Turner had to approve every inch. One year, it was 1949, the year of the Thunderbird, not being happy with any of my various suggestions he said 'come with me' and I followed him into the Drawing Office which was along the passage. Here he took over an unoccupied board and proceeded to design a stand which incorporated the four angled chrome bands which he had introduced at that time as a tank decoration. These surrounded the central fascia and had lighting tubes running the whole length inside. The Triumph logo was added on the outside in the centre and that was it. The contractors, Beck & Pollitzer Ltd, had some problems with the chrome strips because not only were they V-shaped, they had to do a U turn round the fascia at each end. But they managed it and the final job looked fabulous. Such was the genius of the man who ran Triumph at that time. Crankshafts or show stands his flair for design was wide ranging.

The Duke of Edinburgh is escorted round the Triumph stand at the 1952 Earls Court Motor Cycle Show. The lady with glasses to the left of Mr Turner is his intrepid secretary, Miss Nan Plant.

Turner lays down the law to Mr. (now Lord) Boyd-Carpenter MP, a Ministerial visitor at the Earls Court Show of 1955. Jack Sangster listens attentively.

This is the centre piece of the 1949 show stand at Earls Court which Edward Turner himself designed in about half an hour.

Triumph show stands were always very elegant, with dark blue end-to-end carpeting, brilliant lighting and high quality detail. They had to reflect the image of the motorcycle itself.

Vast crowds attended the Earls Court Shows after the war and here is one of them in 1953. They are watching the official opening ceremony.

Another view of the dense crowds, this time on the Triumph stand in 1956. A stand attendant's life was not easy under these conditions.

In 1951 Mr Sangster called us together to tell us that in view of the death duties situation he had felt obliged to sell Triumph to the BSA Group. This came as a shock but with Edward Turner in charge still, there was little chance that Small Heath would interfere in Triumph affairs, and neither did they. In fact there was no noticeable difference in the way Triumph operated and we still competed with BSA as hard, if not harder than before.

For about two years, at the end of the fifties, the BSA board put the Daimler Company under Triumph management and I found that I had become Advertising Manager of that illustrious organisation in addition to my motorcycle committments. This fine old company had not made a profit for some years but Edward Turner soon altered this. All the surplus fat was lopped off and in two short years the company was in profit and was promptly sold to Jaguar much, I believe, to Turner's disgust. He reworked the Daimler range very quickly, modernising the body shapes at minimum cost and designing two splendid V8 engines of $2\frac{1}{2}$ and $4\frac{1}{2}$ litres respectively with cylinder head configurations based on the Triumph Thunderbird. An impressive sight was the first prototype $2\frac{1}{2}$ litre V8 running on the brake, with eight Amal motorcycle carburetters. This beautiful little engine was fitted into a fibreglass bodied sports car known as the SP250. It was to be launched at the New York Show and I was given the job of producing a full colour folder and delivering it to New York in six weeks. This almost impossible task was completed on schedule, with much blood and sweat being expended on the way. As usual, when ET demanded something, he got it, even when it was quite impossible by normal standards.

Edward Turner with the car men at the press preview of the new 3.8 litre Daimler 'Majestic' saloon. Left to Right H.Hastings (The Motor), A.E.Butler (Dunlop), G.J.Long (Daimler Sales Mgr), E.Turner, A.Griffiths (Dir & Gen Mgr), C.M.Simpson (Chief Engineer).

One reason why it was often possible to pull off these miracle jobs was the cooperation we used to get from our suppliers, — studios, blockmakers, printers and so on. And the reason for this was simple. It was a cast iron rule of Charles Parker's finance department that all bills were paid at the end of the month, so that a supplier, asked to do something impossible would pull out all the stops, knowing that he was going to get his money promptly. How different is the situation today when it seems to be a matter of honour amongst accountants generally to see how long they can avoid paying bills. I think that the policy of living on someone else's money is totally immoral, not to mention disastrous to small companies whose cash flow cannot cope with such tactics.

It was at this point that the Managing Director finally conceded that I could probably do with some help and I was permitted to engage an assistant, one Philip Cross who came from Self Changing Gears in Coventry. Phil and I became good friends and worked closely together until he finally took over when I moved into Marketing at BSA Group Headquarters some years later.

'Functions' were part of my responsibility and these usually took the form of press parties, dealer gatherings or retirement parties. The guest lists always caused a lot of 'aggro', with the Managing Director going down the list of names with a jaundiced eye and deleting all those people he did not like or whom he thought should not be entertained at our expense. Sometimes we slipped them back in where we had a special reason and hoped that he would not notice on the night, which was usually the case I am glad to say. Our biggest function was the Overseas Distributors Banquet, always held at the Dorchester Hotel in London. This was a tremendous gathering with guests from all over the world and it highlighted the world wide

Edward Turner on his feet at a Dorchester Export Banquet. Jack Sangster scratches his head.

responsibilities of the little Triumph organisation at Meriden. These people, of all countries, creeds and colours, earned their living selling our products and this party brought home to you, as nothing else could, what the business was all about. Although the Triumph management had a name for looking after the pennies, they could never be accused of skimping on something which was worthwhile and this applied to the Dorchester Banquet. It was superbly staged right down to the last detail and was much enjoyed by all who were lucky enough to attend.

Would-be world travellers are a curse to the publicity departments of any company that makes vehicles and Triumph was no exception to this. Virtually every week we would get a letter from some sanguine character saying that he proposed to ride a motorcycle round the world and after considering all the different available makes he had chosen Triumph because of its great reputation for performance and reliability. This being so and because of the staggering publicity that would result, he was confident that we would see our way to supplying a fully equipped motorcycle, free of charge, and servicing it throughout the journey, also free of charge, of course.

Way back in the twenties there might have been merit in something of this kind, but today a lone motorcyclist sweating his way across India or gasping for breath over the high Andes rates no space in the media when journeys to the moon are a yawn. This fact never seems to be appreciated by these enthusiasts and their numbers never get less – week in, week out, they write and I do not doubt that companies like Land Rover get three times as many as the bike companies.

The usual response was a polite refusal, with an added comment to the effect that the publicity value of such a trip was really negligible under present day conditions, but if the writer did in the end use a Triumph we would be happy to supply a list of our overseas distributors where spares and service could be expected, etc, etc. That was usually the end of the matter and no more was heard.

However there was one trip we did get involved in which contradicts to some extent what I have said. Although it happened some years later than the period generally covered by this book, it is worth mentioning as it was a real epic.

The letter this time was slightly different – it was on the heading of *The Sunday Times* and the writer signed himself Ted Simon. The heading caused me to hesitate when about to dictate the usual reply. I recalled that the editor of *"The Sunday Times"*, Harold Evans, was a keen motorcyclist, so I changed the letter and asked Mr Simon to contact me. This he did and he impressed me at once as being the sort of chap who might well carry something like this right through. The fact that he was a writer, not an enthusiastic motorcyclist, also weighed in his favour. His knowledge of motorcycling was in fact, slight, but his intention was to write a book about the people he met, their way of life and their philosophies, and a motorcyclist would be accepted more readily by the type of person he wanted to meet rather than someone in a car. His story would appear in *The Sunday Times* as he went along.

This settled it for me and I persuaded the management to loan Ted a police type 500 with low compression pistons. I was impressed by his business-like approach to the job. He borrowed a bike for a month to familiarise himself with it, followed by two weeks in the Repair Shop at the works stripping and rebuilding it.

He set out one dull morning with the bike almost buried in gear and four years later he returned, all in one piece, likewise the bike. His quite remarkable story did appear at intervals in *The Sunday Times,* he did write a book and it was published. Everything he promised he did, and the book "Jupiter's Travels" is an extraordinary story, superbly written.

Which all goes to show that there are always exceptions to every rule and Ted Simon's story may serve as an inspiration and a guide to future would-be world travellers on two wheels.

Ted Simon, world traveller extraordinary, with his faithful 500. His journey took four years, he covered over 60,000 miles on the road and survived war, revolutions, accidents and imprisonment.

Finally, a word about Triumph's longest running publicity medium – the White Helmets, or to give them their full title, The Royal Corps of Signals Motor Cycle Display Team. Surely the most famous display team in the world, the White Helmets have been in existence for over fifty years now and have been Triumph mounted right from Day One. The number of different models they have used in this time is legion. They give displays in all parts of the world and are regular performers at the Royal Tournament in London.

Being an ex-member of the Corps myself, I have always taken a particular interest in their affairs, well appreciating the value to Triumph of the exposure the marque gets to tens of thousands of people, captive audiences, every season.

Every year the bikes of the Royal Signals Display Team (known today as the White Helmets) spent the winter in the Meriden repair shop being overhauled by their own mechanics. When they collected the bikes in the Spring it was often the custom to have a little fun on the lawn in front of the factory. Here we see Sales Manager Neale Shilton doing a balancing act. The bikes are 500cc sv twin TRW's.

Chapter Eleven

Post-war developments

*The 1946 3T de Luxe 350 twin. It should have been launched in 1939, when war broke out. A front cover advertisement in **The Motor Cycle** had already been printed and had to be scrapped and done again. The photograph shows a rear Spring Wheel but this was never supplied for 350's.*

The Tiger 85, a proposed sports version of the 3T that was never made – demand for the 500's was too heavy. Many years later a Tiger 90 (350) was produced but this was developed from the unit-construction 3TA.

Something of a stir was caused in two-wheeled circles at the end of 1945, when Triumph plumped for an all-twin range. There was at one time the intention to continue the WD 3HW 350 ohv in civilian guise, painted black, and a leaflet was produced to publicise it, but the model itself never went into production. Demand for the twins overtook it. The 3HW was an attractive single, having the cylinder head cast with integral rocker boxes similar to the 350 twin and those with experience of using it in competition often declared that it was better

The one that started it all, the Speed Twin in post-war guise with four gallon tank and telescopic forks, but the same amaranth red (love lies bleeding) finish.

The engine of the 1946 '3T de Luxe'
55 × 73.4mm 349cc ohv vertical
twin. The rocker boxes were cast
integrally with the head.

than the pre-war Tiger 80. However it was not to be, and it joined the scrap heap along with the three Tigers, 70, 80 and 90, their 'touring' equivalents, the 2H, 3H and 5H and the 350 and 600cc side valves. For the first time in its history, Triumph no longer included a side valve or a single in the range – shades of the old 'Trusties'.

The new range comprised the 350 3T twin, revived from its near debut in 1939, the Tiger 85, a sporting version of the 3T which, in fact, never saw the light of day, the Speed Twin and, of course, the Tiger 100. The latter was a somewhat subdued version of its pre-war counterpart, detuned to run on what passed for petrol at that time. There was not much change in any of these models compared to pre-war, apart from the adoption of telescopic forks, which certainly cleaned up the front end and made a marked improvement in rider comfort. Production was difficult, of course, as the country strove manfully to get back to a peacetime footing. Supplies were erratic but somehow the track kept going most of the time and the new models found their way to the shops, slowly at first but in every increasing quantities as time went on. The public loved them; it was exciting to see the amaranth red (or 'ammer and thread' as some customers called it) Speed Twins, the silver sheen Tiger 100's and the glistening black 3T's after six years of khaki. Demand was high and dealers clamoured for supplies. Bill Johnson in Pasadena, with Edward Turner's very active encouragement, soon got busy and bikes began to flow across the Atlantic in every increasing numbers to develop what very quickly became Triumph's biggest market – the USA. I joined the company at this time as Publicity Manager and had resurrected my pre-war six stud Speed Twin from the shed where it had rested ever since I had departed to the Far East in 1942 to re-inforce the 14th

Yet another non-starter, the 3H, civilian version of the wartime 3HW. There was no manufacturing capacity left if the more profitable demand for the twins was to be met.

Army in its attempts to drive the Japanese out of Burma. The Army succeeded eventually but the Japs got their revenge later by chasing us out of the motorcycle industry. The old Speed Twin started up second kick but I must admit that the clutch plates, in true Triumph fashion, were even stickier than usual after three years of inaction. This bike served me well and I covered a big mileage on it, but on Edward Turner's instruction (but at my expense.) I had to swap it for a 1946 tele forked model more befitting to a member of the Triumph senior management. Incidentally, most of these gentlemen rode motorcycles at this time, either regularly or occasionally. It came as no surprise to see the Chief Buyer or the Company Secretary belting up the Birmingham Road on a Tiger 100 or some other quick model.

The first piece of real excitement in the immediate post war period was the 1946 Manx Grand Prix in the Isle of Man. This was the first race to be held on the mountain circuit since 1939, the TT proper not restarting until 1947. The race was won by an Irishman, Ernie Lyons, on a specially prepared Tiger 100. Built by ex-Brooklands ace Freddie Clarke, who was then head of the Experimental Department, this machine sported an alloy head and barrel from the RAF Generator Set grafted on to a T100 crankcase. It also had the new Spring Wheel rear suspension, an ingenious device designed by Turner which converted a rigid back end to sprung simply by changing the wheel. As the amount of movement was strictly limited, the best that can be said about the Spring Wheel was that it was an improvement on a rigid back end but in no way did it match up to the swinging fork rear ends which were developed some years later. Lyons led from start to finish and won comfortably, despite suffering a broken front down tube on the last lap. Our efforts to keep this broken frame away from the cameras of the

Spring Wheel rear suspension, a Triumph patent which converted a rigid bike to sprung by simply changing the rear wheel. Two Manx Grands Prix were won with it but the movement was very limited and it was ultimately replaced by a conventional swinging fork.

popular press were strenuous in the extreme, likewise the double talk with which we sought to divert attention from it. Weather conditions were appalling and Neale Shilton from our sales force, and myself, watched the race from a wall at Union Mills, completely unaware that we were getting soaked through, such was our excitement as Lyons swept past to victory. His bike served as a prototype for the Grand Prix model which came out for the 1948 season. This retained the alloy head and barrel and also the spring wheel which had, by then, been put into production and was available as an extra on the 500's. The alloy head and barrel also featured on the Trophy model which had been developed for the ISDT.

The following month Lyons put the cat among the pigeons yet again by having the impertinence to collect the trophy for the fastest time of the day at the classic Shelsley Walsh Hill Climb, hitherto the prerogative of the four-wheelers. On Turner's instructions I organised a celebration dinner for Ernie Lyons to be held at the Bath Hotel in Leamington Spa. This was held on the evening of the Shelsley Walsh event, really to mark the victory in the Island, but Ernie's win at Shelsley came as a bonus on the night. Unfortunately Ernie was so late getting back from the hill climb that did not have time to change and this is the only occasion I have ever been to a dinner where the guest of honour sat down to eat in racing leathers.

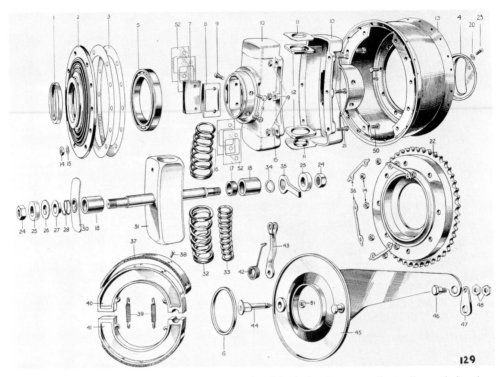

The inside of the Spring Wheel. Not as complicated as it looks but it was unwise to dismantle it unless you really knew what you were doing; it could be dangerous.

Ernie Lyons, the Irish farmer who won the 1946 Manx Grand Prix on a Triumph under appalling weather conditions. He led from start to finish.

Ernie Lyons' Manx winning Tiger 100, which became the prototype for the Grand Prix model introduced for 1948.

Nearside view of the Ernie Lyons bike.

Lyons leaving Governors Bridge. Some idea of the dreadful weather conditions can be judged from this picture.

Lyons rounding Governors Bridge.

Lyons flat out at Sulby.

Attended by Fred Clarke, Lyons prepares to start his record breaking run up Shelsley.

Lyons going well on Shelsley.

Lyons with the Triumph well cranked over on Shelsley.

The Shelsley 'Fastest Time of the Day' Trophy won by Lyons and his Triumph at the October meeting 1946.

Ernie Lyons and Edward Turner at the Manx GP celebratory dinner – held quite by coincidence on the day of the Shelsley Walsh Hill Climb.

'For he's a Jolly Good Fellow' at the Manx GP celebratory dinner for Ernie Lyons, held at Leamington Spa.

In 1949, with the announcement of the new 650cc 'Thunderbird', the launching of which is described later in this book, came some interesting styling changes. The separate headlamp was scrapped and the lamp unit incorporated into what was called a 'nacelle', a technical term borrowed from the aircraft industry. This was a handsome shell and it not only enclosed the lamp unit but the ammeter and lighting switch were mounted on it, as was the speedometer. It surrounded the handlebar mounting clips and the steering damper. The net result was the cleaning up of what is at best a very untidy area of the motorcycle. It was received with mixed feelings, particularly by the diehards, but was rapidly accepted. It certainly made the job of cleaning easier. The Triumph Owners Club adopted 'Nacelle' as the title of their club magazine. Other manufacturers, as always when Triumph brought out something new, attempted to do likewise but their efforts were in no way as eyeable as the original. The removal of the ammeter and switchgear from the tank top left that area clear for a neat little parcel grid, offered as an extra at first, but becoming standard later. Gone too were the chromium panels on the tank sides, (chrome was 'difficult' at that time) to be replaced by four chrome bands with the famous logo mounted thereon. The elimination of these panels not only saved cost but simplified tank production, even if it did reduce the 'showroom glitter' quite a lot. The nacelle lasted well into the sixties, when it was finally overtaken by the demand for 'race track' styling, and the separate headlamp was restored.

The classic beauty of the Triumph. The nacelle completely cleaned up the previous untidy handlebar clutter. All the lines merge in graceful curves and even the front number plate is a thing of beauty. The 1949 Thunderbird.

What better example is there of clean functional motorcycle design that this 1949 Triumph? A place for everything and everything in its place, neatly.

The Army used large numbers of motorcycles in both wars but the demand faded, naturally enough, in peacetime. Nevertheless the authorities continued to work on motorcycle development and one of the results was the Triumph 500cc TRW model. This was a sidevalve twin in what was a close approximation to the Trophy frame. This penchant for side valve engines was a peculiarity of the War Office and Meriden had to design one especially for the purpose, so, being Meriden, they made it a twin. One can almost imagine some ageing brasshat in a Whitehall office somewhere recalling his misspent youth when a burn up the road on his new fangled ohv resulted in the exhaust valve dropping in. This theory is probably way out but remember the Admiralty took an awful lot of convincing that steam was superior to sail. So a side valve it had to be and a very nice little bike resulted. But it was hardly in the "Tiger" class for performance, the engine producing a modest 16·8 hp at 5000 rpm, with a compression ratio of 6 : 1. Two interesting specification items were the Lucas AC Lighting Ignition unit, with a crankshaft-mounted alternator (the first ever, apart from the blitzed Triumph 3TW of 1940) and the Solex 26 WH-Z carburetter. 107 mpg at 30 mph was claimed. The TRW was, of course, submitted to a very thorough testing programme by the Fighting Vehicles Research and Design Establishment at Chobham before it was approved for service use. This included 20,000 miles of night and day riding over all sorts of terrain. Odd to think that in 1913 Mauritz Schulte was playing with a side valve vertical twin – 36 years later Edward Turner, of all people, put one into production. Strangely enough, in the end the British Army ordered only a handful of TRW's but overseas forces, notably Canada and Pakistan, had quite large fleets. The RAF also had a quantity, painted grey of course.

The TRW military machine with its 500cc sidevalve engine. Although produced for the British authorities, the big buyers came from overseas.

The smart little sidevalve engine of the TRW military motorcycle of 1949. It produced a modest 16.8 horsepower.

A rare bird! A TRW with swinging fork rear suspension, believed to be the only one of its kind. It was built in 1957.

A nasty accident? No, a simple way to provide the basis for a riders eye view drawing of the controls for the users handbook.

The Thunderbird had been introduced to meet the never ending demand from the USA and elsewhere for yet more performance and this resulted in the next stage of 650cc development, the T110. This was introduced in 1954 and incorporated a full range of 'go faster' components, bigger valves and ports, higher compression, rather fancy camshafts and other things all fitted into a swinging fork frame.

1954 also saw the 'Terrier' join the range. This neat little 150 ohv was supplemented the following year by a 200cc version known as the 'Tiger Cub'. These lightweights were soon taken up by the trials team and were developed to ISDT standards.

Going back to the big machines, although the T110 was good for around 115 mph and a two carb alloy head could be bought to improve on this, the ultimate 650 just had to come. The bike that would include just about everything that had been learned, often painfully, over many, many years. It did come, at the end of 1958, so late that it missed the 1959 season catalogue. Its name? The Bonneville 120.

This soon became the flagship of the Triumph fleet and established a tremendous record for performance and reliability, a point that was rammed home finally when Malcolm Uphill clocked a 100 mph lap in the process of winning the Production TT in 1969. This was the first time that a production bike had exceeded the magic three figures.

It was just at this time that the three cylinder Trident began to take over – the 'Tiger 100 and a half' as it was known. The Trident is really outside the scope of this book but its impact was tremendous and it set the racing scene well and truly alight in the early seventies. A selection of photographs of this period have been included in the Picture Gallery at the end of the book, but the full story remains to be told.

Before it was possible to build an actual prototype, Edward Turner had this drawing made by Roy Coombs so that he could see what the Terrier would really look like. Compare it with the photograph of the first prototype. Note also the elegant mudguarding, which was obviously abandoned somewhere along the line.

This is the first prototype of the Terrier – the one that would not start first time out. Tank badges are yet to come, but it is fairly complete otherwise.

The bike that looks as if it is doing 70 when it is standing still. The Bonneville of course.

Chapter Twelve

The American market

Author's note; The United States became Triumph's most important market and for many years absorbed the major portion of the factory output. The following account of the history and development of this market is told by Don Brown, the Senior Marketing and Sales Executive for nearly ten years with the Johnson organisation on the West Coast.

In the mid-thirties Triumph was selling a few machines in America through about twelve factory direct dealers whose main lines were either Harley or Indian. Ariel, BSA and Calthorpe machines were handled by British-American Motors operating out of a very small, not especially attractive, facility in Los Angeles. There was no serious effort to expand sales beyond the few odd retail sales which were being made by the owner, Bill Gibson. British bikes were still something of a novelty.

In 1937, William E. 'Bill' Johnson Jr., a bright, gregarious attorney, happened to be in Hawaii when he spotted a 600cc Ariel Square Four parked in front of a store. Bill wasn't a motorcyclist per se but he had a fierce love for machinery and he was always in awe of people who could design things that looked good and worked too. He acquired the address of the factory from the owner and upon returning to the States he learned about British-American Motors and acquired his first motorcycle in Los Angeles. Bill was taken by the unique design concept of the Square Four and it was inevitable that he would eventually take up correspondence with its designer, Edward Turner. At the time Bill was practising law in Los Angeles but in a short time he became so fascinated with his new 'toy' that he bought British-American Motors for the reported sum of $1800. While accounts differ, it seems certain that Bill's first thought was to ensure a source of spares while any thought of serious business was secondary. When Bill bought out the company, the owner Bill Gibson, remarked, 'Hell, you can make the rent from the coke machine proceeds.'... he wasn't far wrong since there was probably more bench racing than business at that time.

While there is no direct record, later accounts of what immediately followed credit Edward Turner's influence on Bill Johnson with persuading Johnson to seriously consider making a full-time project of his newly acquired business. In any case. Bill changed the company's name to Johnson Motors Inc. and moved the operation to a rather fancy facility (for its time) in Pasadena. The place had more glass than walls, or so it seemed, and one story has it that a noted Harley Davidson dealer, Dudley Perkins, made a special trip from Northern California to see the place and was greeted by a man in a white shop coat pushing a mop. Dud's first comment was 'The character who is running this place must be crazy — he'll surely go broke'. The 'character' was Bill Johnson who dryly replied 'You may be right!'

But it wasn't long before Bill began to show his flare for sales promotion. He persuaded all his competitors to join with him in a motorcycle show and invited the public. Everybody kicked in for promotion and there it was — probably America's first consumer exposition for motorcycles. It was no small thing — an absolutely revolutionary idea for the time ... *hell, you don't cooperate with your competitors*! One of the exhibitors was Hap Alzina, the Western States Indian Distributor. After the event he offered Bill the Indian dealership for Los Angeles, which Bill promptly accepted. Indian was a big deal in those days and it looked like a good commercial opportunity. So Bill dropped BSA and Calthorpe to concentrate on the more popular Ariel and Indian machines. Almost at the same time, Johnson secured direct sales rights for Triumph in Southern California and he moved the company to Los Angeles. While the Triumph Speed Twin, Edward Turner's new 'baby', had seen its world debut, none of these bikes had gotten to the West Coast. But no doubt the correspondence between Johnson and Turner had whetted Bill's appetite. Here again was a new design concept which surely would have wide appeal. Johnson and Turner had become fast friends by proxy. Turner may have been an engineer but he possessed great powers of persuasion, especially where his self interests were involved, and he saw in the American Bill Johnson an opportunity to broaden his influence in the potentially lucrative American market. When the first Speed Twin arrived

Bill Johnson of Johnson Motors Inc. and Edward Turner. The two men who launched the Triumph motorcycle on its long and successful run in the American market.

Bill Johnson, a great enthusiast for racing of all types is here seen with **Buck Smith** *at a National Championship Cross Country Event in the early sixties. The machine is a Triumph TR6.*

in America, in 1939, it was an instant success on the racetrack. Aside from its unique vertical twin design, this new machine made a sound so different from anything else on the market. The Ariel Square Four had a similar effect on people, but nothing matched the efficacy of the Speed Twin whine!

There next emerged the first rumblings of philosophic differences between ET and his American associates. The easiest and most natural form of promoting sales of the new Speed Twin was by racing. But ET warned Johnson that racing was a sure road to bankruptcy. Turner believed that the American market, as others, could be manipulated to prevent the necessity of deviating from standard specifications, contributing to special events – or building 'factory specials'. But the Americans were mavericks and ET got just a taste of what was to develop into a life-long contest, when the Johnson organisation began to win consistently in the American style dirt-track TT racing in California. Johnson became fascinated with racing and it was at this time that he hired as a mechanic, Ed Kretz, already a legend in racing with the Indian factory.

Johnson Motors magnificent showroom on Colorado Blvd, Pasadena, California in 1958. Definitely in the Cadillac class!

World War 2 put a damper on business as England was immediately consumed with its urgent defence. Bill Johnson, with the assistance of his associate, Austin Elmore, a well-connected politically oriented fellow, established Johnson Motors as a defence subcontractor. The company, with Elmore's help, had no difficulty in securing contracts, so the firm and its staff continued. Racing even continued during the early years of the war. Out of the records of that era comes the name of Bruce Pierson, 'Boo-boo' Pierson, who literally dominated racing with his Speed Twin in Southern California during the period 1939/42.

When the war was over, Edward Turner went to America. He was in search of new markets and he liked what he saw in California. Bill Johnson and Edward Turner became instant friends. The two men had a lot in common – and respected each other for what the other didn't have. Johnson was a lawyer, a Stanford University graduate, and was 'well connected'. His sister Florence was married to Foster Salzbury, manufacturer of the Salzbury centrifugal clutch and the Salzbury scooter, which achieved reasonable success in California immediately following World War 2. The Salzbury clutch is still in production today.

Edward Turner, on the other hand, had shipped out as a merchant seaman as a young man and in his spare time studied engineering with a passion. But Turner had a natural genius for design and a philosophy which he followed ... and preached religiously. It served him and his financial benefactor, Jack Sangster, well for many, many years.

Turner offered Johnson the Triumph distribution rights for the United States in 1946 and Johnson moved the company to its most famous location at Vernon and Colorado Streets in Pasadena, California. Bill's contract was pretty stiff in those days, when you consider he was required to purchase not less than twelve bikes every year! Of course, what Bill Johnson did not know was that Edward Turner had already sold his production elsewhere and it would be some time before he could catch up on any real increase in demand.

Johnson had his new facility completely redone inside and out and it was, without doubt, the most modern in the motorcycle business in America. It looked a great deal more like a current-day Cadillac dealership than it did a motorcycle operation. Johnson Motors Inc was both a distributor and retail dealer for Triumph and Ariel and also handled the American Mustang and Salzbury Scooter as well. Johnson dropped the Indian dealership about this time to concentrate on his new opportunity with Triumph.

The Johnson team soon returned to racing as a primary method of sales promotion. Ted Evans, a senior level executive at North American Aviation, became the 'national' American racing hero for Triumph. He was brilliant and greatly enhanced the Triumph reputation everywhere he went.

Arguments over racing continued between Johnson and ET. It was as Americans some-times say, a 'Mexican stand-off'. By 1946 Class A short track had returned to the States, a racing form quite familiar to English enthusiasts. Greats of the like of world speedway racing champion Jack Milne and his brother Cordy and the American champion Lammy Lamoreaux, were the stars. Another consistent contender of note was E.W. 'Pete' Colman. Wilbur Cedar, Johnson's general manager and secretary-treasurer, became friendly with Colman and in February 1949, Colman joined the Johnson organisation as a 'road-man', e.g., Sales Representative. Johnson had two such men on the road then – together they covered America! Colman was also a tuner of considerable ability and later became Parts Manager and a Senior Executive at Johnson Motors.

DEVELOPMENT IN BALTIMORE

By 1950, Turner was sure that there was much more business to be had and he wanted Johnson to concentrate more on sales and less on racing. He was concerned that the States had not yet achieved a dominant share of British motorcycle production. It was still 'very small beer'. It was quite obvious to him by this time that Johnson's organisation, although effective and efficient in its own area, would never be capable of exploiting the whole vast continent of America. California is a long way from that bulk of population which inhabits the north east, the east central areas, the south eastern states and the Atlantic seaboard, so the obvious move was to set up some kind of organisation on the Eastern side. At this point Edward Turner called in Percival White, who was President of The Market Research Corporation of America, who happily, was also an enthusiast for motorcycles. White's organisation backed Turner's view that there was a very large potential market for British type motorcycles in America. By another happy coincidence, Percival White's Vice President in charge of European accounts was an ex-patriate Englishman born in Coventry, Denis McCormack. Using their not inconsiderable powers of persuasion, Turner and Sangster secured the release of McCormack who took on the job of President of the newly formed Triumph Corporation, a wholly owned factory subsidiary, with its headquarters in Baltimore.

McCormack, working from scratch, rapidly built up the nucleus of a staff who served him well for many years. Earl Miller, an astute Accountant. Rod Coates, Service Manager and lately winner of the Daytona Amateur 100 race on a Triumph. Jack Mercer, road-man extraordinary, previously employed by Hap Alzina. Phillis Fansler, Office Organiser had been at Bendix with McCormack. Finally John Wright, Lawyer, to steer the new company through the legal jungles. Johnson was not entirely happy about this new arrangement but was obliged to agree since the promotion and servicing of sales in a country the size of America would require more capital than he was willing or able to risk. It was not a happy decision for Turner either, but he was convinced, as was Jack Sangster, that dividing up the country would benefit all concerned in the long term. As subsequent events would confirm, he was absolutely right.

Rod Coates, Service Manager Triumph Corporation (extreme left) and Jack Mercer, Road Man (extreme right) with a cheery group of customers.

The Triumph Corporation had to work in more or less virgin territory for Triumph, in the East. To add to their problems, Harley-Davidson, furious that their comfortable monopoly was being challenged, and by foreign interests at that, had placed pressure on their dealers not to handle Triumph or any other brand. The result of this was that McCormack had to look around for entirely new people and found many of them in the ex-service men seeking some way to invest their gratuities. He also picked up some Indian dealers, that once great company having all but expired. Training schools were held to teach not only Triumph service and repair work but the basics of running a business, finance, stocking, promotion etc. And eminently successful they proved to be. Johnson Motors set up the same procedures in the West and it became a regular annual routine for Edward Turner and senior personnel from the home factory to attend these schools to back up the local instructors and dispense the latest information from headquarters.

It was about this time that Johnson made arrangements with a very talented cross-country racer, Bud Ekins, of Hollywood, California. Bud had been winning on AJS and Matchless models and was given a ride on a 500cc Triumph Trophy for the 1955 Catalina Grand Prix, which he won in record time. He set a new record for the 10 mile circuit for ten laps that beat the old record by nearly ten minutes. For Johnson Motors, the event was a fantastic success because Frank DuBois on an Ariel placed second and Hazen Bair placed first in the 60 mile event on a 165cc Triumph Terrier and Don Hawley won the 200cc event aboard a Tiger Cub. 1955 proved to be a banner year for Triumph. Sal Scirpo riding a Trophy scrambler and sponsored by Triumph Corporation won the famous Eastern Jack Pine Enduro which was con-

Bud Ekins, celebrated American cross-country star, after winning the Catalina Grand Prix in 1955. Note the superb trophy – the bike is a Trophy (model) too. *(Don Brown)*.

sidered to be the toughest enduro course in America. Almost simultaneously, Ed Kretz Jr (son of the famous Ed Senior), won the Peoria, Illinois professional TT National Championship on a Triumph T110. But the really big story was the achievement by Johnny Allen, a soft-spoken slender young Texan, who stepped into a 650cc Triumph-engined streamliner on the Bonneville salt flats, to set a two-way landspeed record for motorcycles of 193 mph. The streamliner, a new concept in record breakers, was designed by 'Stormy' Mangham, a 49 year old American Airlines pilot; the engine, a standard cast iron 650 cc twin was put together by Jack Wilson, Triumph dealer from Texas, while those responsible for negotiating with all the necessary officials, riders, tuners etc were Wilbur Cedar and Pete Colman of Johnson Motors. When the record was set, Bill Johnson stated 'Anyone who wants to beat us will have to beat us by more than 20 mph ... with minor changes in design we can boost our figure to 230 or even 240 mph'. It so happened that in the following year the German NSU factory with a great fanfare of trumpets and a plane load of journalists, set a record of 211.40 mph with a 500cc supercharged twin, only to have Johnny Allen and his team make 214 mph a few days later, after the Germans with their trumpeters had returned home. Their chagrin must have been intense even though Allen's record was not, in the end, officially recognised by the FIM. This led to considerable hostility between the ruling body and the Meriden factory. The objections were purely technical and only related to the absence of an FIM timekeeper. No one doubted the authenticity of the speeds which were achieved. Not that the Americans were worried about the FIM; at that time they were hardly aware of that august body's existence. However, in 1962, another streamliner built by Joe Dudek and 'driven' by Bill Johnson (no relation) achieved 224.57 mph using a 650cc Bonneville engine running on alcohol. This *was* recognised by the FIM.

Johnny Allen signing the Visitors Book in the Lord Mayor's Parlour, Coventry, after his record breaking 193 mph run on the Utah Salt Flats in 1955. With him are L to R Denis McCormack, Bill Johnson, The Lord Mayor, Edward Turner, Neale Shilton, A.J.Mathieu, J.McDonnell and Wilbur Cedar.

The team behind the record breaker in 1955. L to R Jack Wilson, 'Stormy Mangham', Wilbur Cedar, Bill Johnson, John Bough and Johnny Allen.

The moment before the 'off'! The back-up team push the gleaming streamliner into position.

In 1956 Johnny Allen increased his speed to 214 mph and again went to England where his machine was displayed on the Triumph stand at the Earls Court Motor Cycle Show. Here he is being presented with a water colour painting of the run by Robert B.Parke (1st Secty. US Embassy). Also in the picture are Edward Turner, Ivor Davies and Jack Wilson.

Johnny Allen's 214 mph record breaker on the Triumph stand at the Earls Court Show.

One of the big problems Triumph and other importers had, in establishing their American market, was the continued hostility of the Harley-Davidson Company, which has been mentioned before. Not only did they pressure their dealers from selling but through their domination of the American Motorcycle Association, the ohv British bikes were limited to 500cc in certain classes of events against the American 750cc sidevalves. In 'TT' Racing (American style), there were no limits to engine size so the British 650's found themselves racing with 1200cc Harleys. None the less, the Triumphs continued to win more professional TT races than all other makes combined and eventually prove their worth in flat track events. But trade politics were a different matter. Harley appealed to the Tariff Commission in Washington in 1952 asking for the 10% duty on foreign motorcycles to be raised to 40% and a quota system set up. The case for the importers was organised by Denis McCormack and Jack Sangster to such good effect that Harley were finally told, much no doubt to their annoyance, to go away and compete in the good old traditional American manner. Likewise, as time went on, the importers gained a fairer share on the councils of the AMA and discrimination against their machines was discontinued.

BROWN JOINS JOHNSON

'In May 1956, I was asked by Bill Johnson to join Johnson Motors (writes Don Brown). I had first met Bill while I was Editor of *Cycle* magazine but at the time of the offer I was producing the first radio show devoted to motorcyling and Johnson Motors was my one and only sponsor. During the period that the radio show was aired, Bill and I became good friends and at lunch one day Bill said that the radio show, while successful, was too costly to continue but he had a suggestion – would I consider joining his staff? I was 26 at the time and the radio show was the most exciting thing I had done, cross-country racing aside. After some thought I decided in favour and was appointed General Sales Manager with the responsibility of organising a renewed marketing and sales effort in the West.

The feeling I got from Bill was that he was under real pressure to establish a more business-like operation, at least comparable to that of the Triumph Corporation which was not only enjoying success but its aggressive business practices such as regular service training schools, dealer meetings etc were paying off. Upon joining the company, I found one 'road man' aged 62. He promptly quit when he learned he had to report to a 26 year old who came to work in a suit and tie! At that time Johnson's staff comprised Bill himself, as President, Wilbur Cedar, General Admin. Manager/Secretary Treasurer, Clarence E. Fleming, Legal Counsel, E.W. 'Pete' Colman, Parts Manager and technical liaison with the factory, Alva A. Martin, Office Accounting Manager.

My first meeting with Edward Turner was in January 1957. Johnson Motors held its dealer meetings in January, not because it made sense, but because the one race Turner immensely enjoyed was the Big Bear Run, the biggest event in the world in terms of the number of entrants – up to 1200 before it was discontinued. The Big Bear was held in January and its start was located about 90 miles north of Los Angeles. Bill Johnson and ET always made a week-end of it and the whole affair was a stimulus to ET because an English bike was bound to win whether or not it was a Triumph. After all, Turner considered himself a representative of the Crown!

One incident I shall never forget. We were all set to attend the Big Bear and with ET was A.J. Mathieu, Triumph's Export manager at the time. Bill invited me to drive, so he and ET

Where else would you get such a picturesque starting place for a race? The Catalina GP 1956. The rider carrying No 60 is Don Brown, who finished 4th in the 350 class.

could relax in the rear of Bill's Cadillac sedan. We went up the day before, stopping at the famous Apple Valley Inn where most of the top racers and industry people watered down. The racecourse formed two giant loops through the desert, traversing some 190 miles and climbing some 7000 feet above sea level; one drove to the midpoint at Lucerne after the start to see the riders come through and then up the mountain to the finish at Fawnskin. This particular time we were doing about 80 mph along a slightly bumpy paved road into Lucerne when Bill and ET got into discussion about the relative merits of British and American cars. It was soon evident that the discussion was getting heated. ET said 'Bill, look at this car – electric doors, electric windows and seats, automatic climate control, electric doorlocks, automatic air suspension – it is full of trouble simply waiting for an inconvenient place to happen'; Bill protested. 'Damn it Ed, there is nothing more unreliable than a British car ... this car hasn't given me one damn bit of trouble ....' ET folded his arms and declared that he would be surprised if we reached our destination on time.

Believe it or not but at that very instant, I felt the car begin to slow down – I pushed on the accelerator to no avail, I fiddled with the ignition with no results. God! ... HAD ET WILLED THE CAR TO QUIT? Sensing the speed change ET leaned up and asked, 'We seem to be slowing down ... any reason?' Oh how I hated to announce that Bill Johnson's favourite 'reliable' Cadillac had in fact quit cold. ET slumped back and in the mirror I could see that familiar grin – he *knew* we were in trouble! Johnson was furious but the car still came to a complete dead stop.

The Johnson Motors pit crew at the 1957 Big Bear cross-country race.

Mathieu and I popped open the hood but couldn't find anything. ET had gotten out and was standing on a ridge of sand looking down at us. 'I know precisely what's wrong, but I don't intend to do a thing about it', he said. 'Aw come on Ed', I pleaded, 'what the hell is wrong?'. 'It's very simple', he replied, 'there's a short somewhere in the primary wiring harness', As it turned out, he was absolutely right, ... was he ever wrong?

I decided to hitch a ride into Lucerne and the first vehicle that came along was a pick up truck with two young men in the cab and a couple of Triumphs in the back. As luck would have it, the driver was a mechanic at a Cadillac dealership in Pasadena and he soon found the trouble; the primary wiring harness had in fact shorted against the frame.

Then it REALLY happened! While under the car, the mechanic said 'How about raising the air suspension to give me some room'. I reached for the handle on the dash but when I pulled it out I almost fell into the back seat ... the handle separated from its cable, the car gave a loud hiss and settled flat onto its frame! The poor guy helping could hardly breathe and Johnson's face was crimson. The mechanic struggled out and I tipped him $20.00. ET stood around with a smug 'I told you so' look on his face. Finally we got going again; Bill's favourite Cadillac rode like a tank, but it did run. Bill Postel on a 650 Triumph won the Big Bear that particular year, and Johnson Motors and Triumph Corporation continued to support active racing programmes and, despite the doubts of Edward Turner, the two companies converted these victories into ever increasing commercial success until the shadow of the Rising Sun loomed over the horizon.

A Triumph at full blast on the dirt! **(Motor Cycle Weekly)**

Don Brown taking the first ever order for $100,000 from retail dealer Bill Robertson Sr of Hollywood, California.

THE BIG TAKEOVER

Edward Turner's 'Report on Japan' can be read later in this book. It is dated 1960 and precisely at this time the Japanese (ie. Honda) moved into the American market. They had a lot of money to spend and they spent it effectively in setting up their organisation and promoting their products. They increased the overall size of the market enormously and introduced motorcycling to a vast number of entirely new customers. That they were able to do this comparatively quickly was in no small measure due to the considerable pool of skilled personnel and dealers created by Triumph over the previous twenty five years. Many senior people and dealers moved into the Japanese camp. But the invasion was not all bad for Triumph and the other British importers. Japanese products at this time were confined to the lightweight end of the market and British importers prospered when the new customers created by the Japanese wanted something bigger and more exciting to ride. But this situation could not last and the introduction of big capacity models from Japan was not long delayed. This, combined with the increasing industrial and financial problems of the British industry in the late sixties and early seventies, led to the run-down of that superb organisation in America which had been created from virtually nothing by the combined genius and hard work of Edward Turner, Jack Sangster, Bill Johnson, Denis McCormack and their dedicated staffs on both sides of the Atlantic.

*Bud Ekins (500 Triumph) has a hectic moment on his way to winning the Open Class in the Catalina Grand Prix **(Don Brown)**.*

Stylish cornering by Bud Ekins on a TR5 in the Catalina Grand Prix. On this occasion he retired with a flat tyre.

A good shot of Denis McCormack and Edward Turner at Baltimore. The plaque commemorates the opening of the Triumph Corporation headquarters.

When Edward Turner added Managing Directorship of Daimler Cars to his responsibilities in the late fifties, the Triumph Corporation became distributors for these famous cars. L. to R. Denis McCormack, Edward Turner, Earl Miller, Jack Wickes.

Bud Ekins outside the Triumph factory at Meriden prior to going to Germany for the ISDT.

Some of the winning Triumph riders in the 1962 Jack Pine 550 miles — 472 entries — 175 finishers. Every engine category was won by Triumph.

In September 1962 a 38 year old truck driver, Bill Johnson, averaged 224.57 mph at Bonneville Salt Flats with a streamliner design by Joe Dudek round a 650 Triumph Bonneville engine, and set a new world record.

The Joe Dudek projectile getting a push start. The canopy over the driver is fitted later.

Bill Johnson explains the streamliner to Edward Turner outside the Triumph factory at Meriden.

Johnson and Dudek being presented with silver Tudor Rose dishes in recognition of their 224 mph world record.

Disaster on the salt! In 1959, Johnny Allen made another attempt on the record in his famous streamliner 'No 18'. At 220 mph and still accelerating the parachute ropes locked the rear wheel! Allen held it for about 500 yards and it then rolled and flipped for a further half mile. Allen walked away with some broken ribs, cuts and bruises!

Busy scene on the salt flats prior to Allen's spectacular crash. Bill Johnson and Clarence Fleming Jr. man the cameras.

Desert racing was a favourite sport of movie star Steve McQueen – Triumph was his favourite bike.

Over 230 dealers attended this Convention at Baltimore in 1963. On the front row we recognise Jack Mercer, Denis McCormack, Edward Turner, Earl Miller, John Nelson (Service Mgr from Meriden), and Rod Coates.

E.W. 'Pete' Colman of Johnson Motors shakes hands with Triumph Director Charles Parker, with Pete's wife Marilyn and Bert Hopwood behind. Earls Court 1963.

Chapter Thirteen

Success breeds sales?

In the promotions budget of every motorcycle company there is a heading entitled 'Competitions', because sales promotion is what competitions are all about. This is a point often misunderstood by enthusiasts who imagine that companies go racing or scrambling because they enjoy it. Very often they do, but this is not the reason they do it. They do it to try and sell more motorcycles. Now whether sales follow success has never been proved beyond all doubt but comparatively unknown foreign companies have indisputably registered their existence very strongly by a successful onslaught on the race circuits. But, and this is the crux of the matter, they backed it up with sound products at the right price, with service and customer satisfaction. There have been UK manufacturers who could win races but their performance in the market place often nullified the success of their racing.

Triumph supported off-road competitions quite strongly for many years after the war and later was a star performer in the production road racing field. At the same time the product and service was first class so the sales package was complete.

Some of our adventures are described in this and following chapters.

THE OFF-ROAD GAME

In Coventry trials riding and scrambling circles after the war the name of Jim Alves kept appearing at the top end of the results sheets. Riding a Velocette MAC, suitably reworked, Jim obviously knew what the game was about. For scrambling he used a Triumph ex-WD 3HW and was a consistent winner.

Triumph at this time had been too busy getting into production after the War to worry about competitions but with the big Open Trials re-starting, it was soon obvious that some

Jim Alves testing ENX 674, the twin cylinder 350, soon after it had been built.

thought would have to be directed that way. The big snag was that we only had twins in the range and as everyone knew, you had to ride a single to win trials, you could get no grip with a twin. I think it was Jack Welton who first drew our attention to Jim Alves. Jack, a Coventrian born and bred, was well informed on local club matters and activities. His job at Triumph was Sales Office Manager and his service with Triumph dated back to Bettmann days. So Alves was contacted and agreed to try a twin, it would be an interesting experiment. So the Repair Shop got busy (we did not have a Comp Shop in those days) and ENX 674 came into being. This was a stock 3T 350 twin stripped of all surplus equipment, lights etc and with a cut-and-shut 2 into 1 exhaust running along the near side. Jim and I went out with this to Kenilworth Common where, totally illegally, we spent the afternoon riding it up and down the best sections we could find in this beauty spot. Surprise, surprise! The sewing machine-like qualities of the little 350 twin engine seemed ideal for the job — quiet, effortless and very easy to control. No particular problems with grip either, just careful handling of the throttle — could the pundits be wrong? I remember the same argument being levelled against spring frames years later — no way would the back end grip with springs. How wrong can we all be.

Reporting these results back at the factory, Edward Turner became very interested and demanded a demonstration. So an expedition set out to the Cotswolds where we found some *real* sections where the little twin performed just as well as it had at Kenilworth and it was obvious by this time too that Alves was really getting the touch with it. So it got the blessing from the Big White Chief and it was back to the factory once more to really screw little ENX 674 together and make it fit to do battle with our deadly enemies from Small Heath, Selly Oak, Redditch and Plumstead. No doubt they would smile pityingly when they saw us, but we now had no alternative, Turner would never tolerate us using something like an outdated 3HW single which was not in current production.

Our first big event was the Cotswold Cups Trial in 1946 and to the astonishment of every-one Alves romped home a comfortable winner. We were as staggered as the opposition and I remember being set upon by the salesmen of *The Motor Cycle* and *Motor Cycling* demanding copy for a full page advertisement in the following week's issues. Although I was the Advertising Manager I had never imagined this situation would arise so soon and in the haze of the Amberley Inn at Rodborough Common I was desparately trying to evolve some suitable wording which could be telephoned to the presses waiting in London. That was quite a night.

So began the twin cylinder era in competitions and no longer was the effectiveness of the twin questioned. In fact, Billy Nicholson, the celebrated Irish star from BSA, built himself a 500 twin shortly after but as far as I can recall did not ride it very often. When the 1948 International Six Days Trial due to be held in San Remo, Italy, was getting near, once again we had the problem of what to use. The 350 twin was a delightful tool for nadgering round trees and up muddy banks but it lacked the top end performance which would be necessary in the ISDT.

So we looked at the Speed Twin and eventually Henry Vale, our ace ISDT bike builder, (as he turned out to be) built three 500's based on the stock 5T but using the alloy head and barrel from the wartime generator set which had proved so effective on the Ernie Lyons Manx winning bike. The alloy not only reduced the overall weight but the parallel exhaust ports kept the pipes well tucked in and out of harm's way. Three Gold Medals and a Team Prize was the score at the end of the week and everyone was satisfied, except the riders, Alves, Allan Jefferies and Bert Gaymer. Although the bikes had been completely reliable and fast enough, their weight and handling qualities left something to be desired. So out of the inquest came the superb Trophy model, shorter, lighter, with an alloy head and barrel and a dream to handle. It became one of the most desirable of all Triumph models and the scores it chalked up in succeeding ISDT's and thousands of other events underlined its prowess as a competitive motorcycle.

Alves climbs Hollingsclough in the 1946 Bemrose Trial on the new twin.

The 1948 ISDT 500, a much modified Speed Twin. The Triumph team collected three Gold Medals and a Team Prize.

The rider's view of the 1948 ISDT 500. This photograph shows the clock and speedo cable arrangements and the route card holder.

The 1948 Triumph ISDT Team – Allan Jefferies, Jim Alves and Bert Gaymer.
They won three Gold Medals and a Team Prize.

Allan Jefferies in the '48 ISDT in Italy. Allan captained the successful British Trophy Team.

Bert Gaymer leaves a check in the '48 ISDT.

Now a word or two about Jim Alves, (his real names were Percival Harold) who at that time was a quantity surveyor working for Humber Ltd, the car manufacturers in Coventry. A native of Street, Somerset, he returned there later with a reputation as a top rank competition motorcyclist and set up a motorcycle dealership handling Triumph and other makes. This prospered later into the four-wheeled world as an exclusive Volkswagen franchise. Jim was a tireless seeker after perfection and had few equals as an ingenious mechanic. I believe he was the first ISDT star to adopt a heavy safety pin to replace the split pin in the front brake operating arm. A safety pin could be taken out (and put back) in half the time of a split pin. He was always looking for improvements to the bike. I have seen him after an event on a Saturday strip the bike right down, change the head angle on a primitive blacksmiths hearth comprising an upturned dustbin lid in his back garden, rebuild the bike and ride next day. If it did not then feel better, he would put it back to its original condition or some other alternative. At one period he had a 'thing' about the wheelbase and the 3T got shorter and shorter until the wheels were almost touching, when it became unmanageable and Jim and the bike parted company rather hurriedly when out on test. The wheelbase returned to normal next day.

Jim Alves back at the works – the dented tank is one way of getting more steering lock.

National trials involved some extensive travelling and long hours and in the early days after the war I used to go to them all, usually passengering with Jim Alves in his car with trailer behind. At this time money and cars were scarce and Jim had a little pre-war 8hp Ford and with this he used to tow the trailer with two bikes on and usually four bodies in the car. At times the poor little thing was hard pushed to make the tops of quite modest hills and we had a drill to cope with this which worked very well, but must have looked very funny from the roadside. When the revs in bottom gear had dropped to the danger line Jim would shout 'all out' and the three passengers would erupt into the road through the single available door with the car still moving. This enabled the sorely stressed engine to pick up and crawl over the top of the hill where Jim would wait for his passengers to catch up and get in the car again.

When the Tiger Cub made its appearance in the mid-fifties its potentialities as a trials mount were rapidly exploited and the team forsook their twins for the little one. This surely pointed the way in which trials motorcycle development was going to go and today anything bigger than 250cc is virtually unknown.

Allan Jefferies was the doyen of Triumph riders, probably England's greatest all-rounder, equally at home in the Isle of Man as on the Scottish hills. Jefferies started his riding career in the twenties, was taken on by Triumph in 1933 and was still riding after the war, when he captained the successful British Trophy Team in the ISDT and was one of the riders in the Thunderbird test at Montlhéry in 1949. In 1947 and 1949 he finished second in the Club-mans TT in the Island on Tiger 100's. Later, Allan became a tower of strength on the administrative side of the sport and was very active in raising money for the Motor and Cycle Trades Benevolent Fund. And there were plenty of others who made names for themselves at the time. I particularly recall Johnny Giles, Bert Gaymer, Peter Hammond, Roy Peplow, Bob Manns, Jack Wicken, Ken Heanes and Artie Ratcliffe, all of whom I had the privilege of working with as administrator to the Competition Department.

1949 saw the first production TR5 developed from the Speed Twins used in the 1948 ISDT. A beautiful little bike, it was popular for many years.

One of the 1949 works team machines — virtually a standard TR5.

Trophy teams called for various capacity machines, so a Thunderbird 650 engine was slotted into a TR5 chassis in 1951.

The first ISDT model with swinging fork back end. This was a 650.

1953, a fully sprung 500 scrambler with the very pretty fine pitch fin alloy motor.

Our first venture into the trials game with a lightweight. This was a 150cc 'Terrier' built for Alves in 1953.

A prototype 'Trophy' for 1955, with swinging fork back end.

A spring frame Trials 500 built for Jack Wicken in 1954.

The first fully sprung 200cc trials Cub, ridden by George Fisher in the 1956 Scottish.

A 1957 500cc Scrambler for Ken Heanes, with a two carb head.

A Cub Scrambler for Johnny Giles, built in June 1957.

Another 500cc twin carb scrambler with modifications – 2 into 1 exhaust, 8 inch front brake and short seat.

A very special 175cc Cub for the 1957 ISDT.

A Unit 500 built for Roy Peplow for the 1961 ISDT.

The 1960 Trials Cub, a formidable competitor.

A 1960 500 Scrambler – note the vast rear sprocket.

A rude gesture from Alves!

Alves on his 500 in the 1953 Hurst Cup Trial **(Thomas McCleary)**

This could only be the Scott Trial! Alves picks his way through a wet section in 1951. **(Photocraft)**

Alves with his Cub up high somewhere in
the 1954 Scottish. (*Ray Biddle*).

A youthful looking Ken Heanes on a Cub for
the 1958 ISDT.

Ken Heanes blasts his 650 off the line in the Welsh tests for the 1962 ISDT. Heanes built up an incomparable record over many years in the International. **(Motor Cycle News)**.

Ken Heanes scrambling – today one would refer to it as 'moto-cross- but how can you say 'Ken Heanes moto-crossing'?

Artie Ratcliffe negotiates the rocky brook course of Crumpsbrook One in the '57 British Experts. He finished a brilliant fourth on his Cub. **(B.R.Nicholls)**.

The Arctic conditions look anything but funny but Roy Peplow and Johnny Giles manage a laugh.

Peter Hammond in the 1954 ISDT in Wales. The 'spectators' are Edward Turner, Henry Vale and Bill Johnson (President, Johnson Motors USA).

Gordon Blakeway at speed on the 500 unit scrambler. (**B.R.Nicholls**).

*Jack Wicken in a dignified stance in the Welsh Two Day Trial 1953. He won it. (**Ray Biddle**).*

*Johnny Giles negotiating some wicked looking rocks on his 500. Event and location not known. (**Holder & Osborn**)*

Johnny Giles scrambling. (1960)

The Triumph team at the Stroud tests in preparation for the 1955 ISDT. Jim Alves, Johnny Giles and Jack Wicken are all on 500s, built by Henry Vale, who is also in the picture.

Ray Sayer concentrating hard, keeps his feet up.

The Triumph Team for the 1953 Scottish Six Days Trial. Jim Alves, Peter Hammond and Jack Wicken.
(Ray Biddle)

The Triumph Team in the 1949 ISDT held in Wales. L to R Jim Alves, Bob Manns and Bert Gaymer.
(Motor Cycling)

A gathering at the back of the works prior to the 1956 International Six Days Trial. L to R Ivor Davies, Jack Wicken, Johnny Giles, Henry Vale, Ken Heanes, Vic Fidler and George Fisher.

Bob Manns aviating in the 1949 Binley (Coventry) Scramble.

Finally, a word about the bike builders. Henry Vale was in charge of the 'comp shop'. With long years of service at Triumph, Henry was a perfectionist whose record of building reliable machinery must be without equal. A very good rider himself, he knew what was wanted and how to get it. A very forthright individual, he did not suffer fools gladly, and was always ready to argue his point of view. At Six Day events he was invariably in the right place at the right time and I swear he could tell a rider what was wrong with his bike without moving his lips (outside assistance was forbidden). His adventures on the Continent of Europe at various International Six Day Trials would fill a book and the number of gold medals won by Triumph riders when Henry was building and looking after the bikes is a sure testimony not only to the skill of the riders but Henry Vale's ability to build a fast and utterly reliable mount. For a long time he was ably assisted by Vic Fidler, a formidable wielder of spanners who was in some ways as forthright a character as Henry himself. Vic was a great enthusiast who, despite the fact that he spent every day working on bikes, would go off cheerfully at the week-end to look after the bikes of some local grass track or scrambles rider.

Chapter Fourteen

Tribute
to the `GP`

In the Turner era, a love-hate relationship with road racing was almost official policy. Edward would expound 'ad nauseum' on the futility of factories expending their money and best brains on trying to win races when they should be using them for the production of better motorcycles to sell. He would list all the makes which had gone to the wall or were not as prosperous as they might be due to their preoccupation with racing.

To be fair to him, his real objection to racing was its development of specialised machines which bore no relation to anything one could buy in the dealers shop (apart from the name on the tank). He always said that when true production racing was introduced, Triumph would be interested. This came to pass much later as we all know, and Triumph picked up a fair share of the victor's laurels.

We have already described in an earlier chapter how Ernie Lyons won the 1946 Manx Grand Prix on a Tiger 100 which had been carefully put together by Freddie Clarke, who was head of the Triumph Experimental Department at the time. Fred was a pre-war Brooklands star and did some of the Speed Twin engine development on the concrete saucer. He also set the 750cc all-time lap record on a 503cc Speed Twin at 118.02mph, as well as the 350cc record on a Tiger 80, at 105.97mph. Fred was quite a character, habitually taciturn except when celebrating, his analytical approach to problems and his stubborn refusal to accept trigger happy hunches earning him the respect of his colleagues and the confidence of the Managing Director. If he was brooding over some difficulty it was often possible to stand in his shop for ten minutes before he would take any notice of you — if you hadn't given up and left by that time.

Ernie Lyon's winning model was then developed into an over-the-counter racer called, appropriately enough, the 'Grand Prix'. The idea behind it was, to quote from a leaflet that I produced for it at the time''...to enable the non-professional rider to compete on level terms in

This is the production model 'Grand Prix', developed from the 1946 Manx GP winning Tiger 100.

all types of long and short circuit racing''. From the factory point of view it was just another model, a strictly commercial proposition. The bikes were bought, the parts were bought and as they were near standard T100, it caused the minimum of upheaval in the works.

Edward Turner liked to win, but there was an unwritten rule that if a Triumph won we basked in its reflected glory whereas if it lost, or blew up, we disowned it completely. With the introduction of the 'Grand Prix' model it was natural that Senior TT competitors should show some interest and the GP had some good riders on the start line in 1948. Riders like Freddie Frith, Ken Bills, Bob Foster, Vic Willoughby Albert Moule and Syd Barnett. The first two were sponsored (as we should say today) by Nigel Spring, whose name was usually associated with Nortons.The factory, on the face of it, did not appear to be involved and it is probably just as well, as all the Triumph riders retired. However Triumph honour was vindicated later in the year when Don Crossley won the Manx with Reg Armstrong 4th, Arthur Wheeler 5th, C.A.Stevens 7th, and Peter Crebbin and S. Anderton 11th and 12th. In the 1949 Senior TT, Syd Jensen of New Zealand finished 5th with C.A.Stevens 6th and several other finishers lower down. We threw a party for Crossley and the other Manx finishers whilst Syd Jensen was entertained suitably by the Managing Director and other members of the staff.

Albert Moule, Senior TT 1948.

Freddy Frith, Senior TT 1948.

Bob 'Fearless' Foster at Braddan. 1948 Senior TT.

Syd Barnett, of Coventry, takes delivery of a new GP in January 1948. With him are pre-war Rudge stars Ernie Nott and Tyrell Smith, in charge of Triumph Experimental at this time.

Don Crossley after winning the 1948 Senior Manx Grand Prix. Two other well known riders in the group are Ken Bills, left and Ernie Nott, right.

Peter Crebbin, who came 11th on a Tiger 100 in the 1948 Manx GP. Many years later Peter became a regular member of the Travelling Marshals, always riding Triumph.

Reg Armstrong, 4th in the 1948 Manx. Reg later became famous as a works rider, first for AJS, then Norton partnering Geoff Duke and finally Gilera, again with Duke. He won the Senior TT in 1952.

C.A.Stevens, 7th in the 1948 Manx and 6th in the 1949 Senior TT.

The Manx Grand Prix celebration dinner held in Kenilworth in September 1948. L to R S.Anderton (17th), H.R.Armstrong (4th), D.Crossley (1st), P.Crebbin (11th), Edward Turner, C.A.Stevens (7th), and A.Wheeler (5th).

After this the GP faded away. Only about 175 were built in all but I think it is fair to say that the objective of providing a competitive bike for 'non-professional' riders was achieved. Two Manx Grand Prix wins in three years surely proved this. I still reckon the GP to be one of the best looking bikes we ever made. It was not designed to compete with the Manx Nortons and the Porcupines and other very specialised machinery but even so, David Whitworth campaigning a lone GP on the Continent was up with the winners on many occasions.

The GP, as bought, was ready for immediate racing and each was supplied with a certificate giving general data and the horsepower figure attained by the particular engine. We quoted a figure of 120mph as being possible, running on Pool petrol and pistons were also available for petrol-benzole and alcohol fuels. The alloy square finned ex-RAF generator head and barrel were used and these, together with the Dunlop light alloy racing rims and alloy guards, kept the total dry weight down to around 314 lbs, a figure which was good even in those days. The Spring Wheel rear suspension was included in the specification.

I well remember having an unofficial ride on Crossley's Manx winning GP at the Anstey airfield circuit near Coventry. I completed several laps (cap back to front I recall) and to someone familiar only with road bikes it was a shattering experience — as was the noise and acceleration when it 'came on the megga'.

Sid Jensen of New Zealand at the start of the 1949 Senior TT. He finished 5th on his GP.

Sid Jensen of New Zealand and Harry Hinton of Australia (Norton) battle it out in the 1949 Senior TT. Jensen finished 5th, Hinton was 9th.

Jensen with members of the Triumph Senior Staff outside the works. L to R C.W.F. Parker (Secretary), I.G.Davies (Publicity), S.Crabtree (Buyer), S.Jensen, E.Turner, H.Holland (Export), H.G.Tyrell-Smith (Experimental), A.J.Welton (UK Sales), S.N.Shilton (UK Sales).

David Whitworth, who carried out much practical development on the GP model, is here seen at speed in the 1947 Belgian Grand Prix.

Another Belgian Grand Prix shot with Whitworth leading.

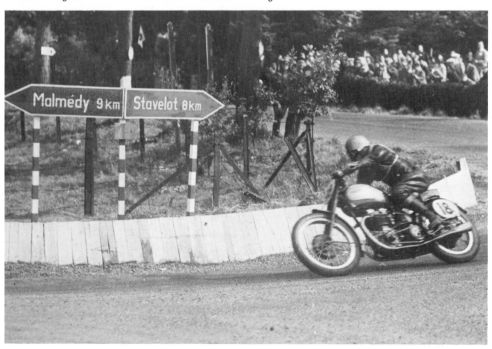

The 1949 Ansty meeting (Coventry), Syd Barnett in full flight.

Another Ansty shot with Syd Barnett and Arthur Wheeler fighting it out.

Bob Foster with his front wheel well off the ground – also at the 1949 Ansty meeting.

Chapter Fifteen

Lands End and all that

The motorcycle industry has always been a firm believer in that old adage 'proof of the pudding etc' and public demonstrations of performance have been powerful weapons in the sales manager's armoury in his fight to persuade the public to buy his product in preference to those of his rivals. They were of vital importance back in the early days when it was an achievement if the average rider managed to return home the same day without any major repair work en route.

The difficulty has always been to devise a demonstration which is novel yet makes the point. Your objective must be absolutely clear whether it be hill climbing, reliability, speed, fuel consumption or whatever. Hill climbing was an obvious one in the days when hills were a real problem for your everyday motorcyclist. Snowdon and Ben Nevis have both been defeated by motorcycles and multiple climbs of Welsh terrors like Bwlch-y-Groes have been popular in both the motorcycle and car industries. Lands End to John O'Groats was another favourite and if the number of runs made between these two points were laid end to end they must surely reach the moon. Some stunts were just pure stunts – like Harry Perrey's famous return crossing of the English Channel on a float-mounted 500cc Ariel. What it proved I was never too sure, but it was great fun. Perrey, in addition to being a formidable competition rider, was probably the most prolific originator of demonstrations on both two wheels and three that the industry has ever known.

Triumph has staged many exploits of one kind or another over the years. In 1911, for example, Mr A.E.Catt (the Harry Perrey of his day) was proclaimed as 'holder of the Six Consecutive Days Record, all-England route, 2557 miles : averaging 426 miles a day'. When you consider the bike he rode – single gear belt drive with 'free engine', this was a fantastic performance by any reckoning. Even more so when you take into consideration the relatively primitive dust laden roads of that era. In the same year, Ivan B.Hart Davies held the Lands End to John O'Groats record, on a Triumph – 29 hours 12 minutes for the 886 miles.

Mr A.E.Catt, a formidable long distance record breaker on Triumph machines in the days before the Great War.

NH-587

MR. A. E. CATT.

Demonstrations are usually 'officially observed' by the ACU and a steward is appointed whose job it is to see that everything is recorded that has any bearing on the objectives of the trip. He is also supposed to see that no sharp practices are indulged in. A story which has been handed down at Triumph concerns a long distance sidecar run in which the ACU steward occupied the sidecar. Came the end of one day and the engine was showing distinct signs of impending doom. The overnight hotel was reached, just, and the outfit duly locked up in the garage until next morning. Fortunately the ACU man was a convivial soul who enjoyed a drink and the Triumph people made sure that he did not go thirsty. He passed peacefully out in due course and was put to bed. Meanwhile the engine had been slipped out of another machine, the garage lock picked, a quick engine change and all was well in the morning — except that the steward complained about an almighty hangover.

Edward Turner's objection to racing as a sales aid was always based on the fact that racing machinery was 'special' and bore no resemblance to the bike that the man in the street could buy. This was true of course, his point being that results achieved by these machines were no help as a decision maker in the showroom. However I was won over to Velocette before the war purely on their TT results. I knew that my KSS was not much like Stanley Woods' KTT but there was a strong family resemblance, they both had black tanks and overhead camshafts.

Turner's policy was never to spend money and talent making specials, it all had to go into the standard product. There was much to be said for this. If racing sold bikes then Nortons with their incomparable record should have been the market leaders of their day but they were not and Triumph outsold them comfortably. But Turner was always keen to demonstrate the stock product and in 1937 three of his new models, the Tigers 70, 80 and 90 won the Maudes Trophy and this achievement was repeated in 1939 with the Speed Twin and new Tiger 100. The Maudes Trophy was a magnificent award, put up by a member of the retail trade for feats of this kind.

Two demonstrations with which I was involved took place in 1949 and 1953. The Speed Twin had been a great success in the United States but now customers there were demanding more and more performance. Long distances, straight roads and the inborn enthusiasm of the American rider made this inevitable. Turner's answer was very simple. He 'stretched' the Speed Twin from 63 x 80mm to 71 x 82, thereby increasing the capacity from 498 to 649cc and putting up the bhp from $26\frac{1}{2}$ to 34. There was enough metal in the Speed Twin barrel to permit this increased bore and one is inclined to think that E.T. might have had this in mind when he decided the dimensions of the Speed Twin engine in the first place. The result was a substantial increase in performance without any increase in weight or real cost for that matter. It did mean we could charge more to the customer which commercially was very satisfactory. Turner told us he had decided to call this new model the 'Thunderbird' which was a lovely sounding name of North American Indian origin.

The engine in my own Speed Twin was changed for one of the experimental 650's during the development stages and the result was startling, yet externally there was no difference. My club mates were vastly puzzled by the shattering performance of my bike – I never let on.

It was decided that we would have to launch the new model in style and weeks of thought were given to this problem. Obviously we had to show how fast the Thunderbird would go but reliability was also important. So it came down to deciding what was the highest speed we could go over the longest distance without risking a blow up. Fortunately we had the services of those two Isle of Man experts, H.G.Tyrell Smith and Ernie Nott, running the Experimental Department at that time. They covered big mileages on the prototypes and finally came up with the suggestion that we ought to be able to crack 500 miles at 90 mph. Turner agreed, but added that three machines would be used just to rub it in.

From a publicity and advertising point of view I was happy – 500 miles sounded a long way and 90 mph was certainly fast. Where to do it was the next problem. MIRA had not been thought of and Brooklands was no more. We would have to go to Montlhéry in France. Neale Shilton, from our sales side, was put in charge of arrangements. It was decided to take four machines (one spare) and these were equipped with panniers and ridden to Montlhéry by Shilton, Alex Scobie, Tyrell Smith and Len Bayliss and they were joined in France by two more well-known Triumph exponents, Allan Jefferies and Jim Alves. Ernie Nott was included among the riders originally, but a locked gearbox during a flat out run down the Meriden 'mile' damaged his shoulder. I saw them off from Meriden and the next few days were anxious ones wondering what was happening. Suddenly late one afternoon my office phone rang and Shilton's voice said 'We've done it – take these figures down'. I wrote the speeds down on a piece of scrap paper which I kept in my wallet for years after. Yes, I was excited, this was my first really big publicity 'do' and my excitement was shared in the factory, where everyone had been waiting for the news. I was then involved in a tremendous spate of hard work with press releases, advertising, and all the thousand and one other things that have to be done on these occasions. Of course most of it had been pre-prepared, so it was now a case of putting in the

The Thunderbird demonstration. The four machines leave the works ridden by (L to R) Len Bayliss, Neale Shilton, Tyrell Smith and Alex Scobie. The date, 16th September 1949.

figures and pressing all the buttons. One of our best creative efforts was the Thunderbird motif – a swooping bird, very stylised, which became highly popular on badges, ties and on the bike itself.

Thunderbird demonstration; the team leaves the works and heads down the Birmingham Road towards London. Note the gear being carried, including tyres.

Thunderbird demonstration – the entire 'establishment'. (L to R) Edward Turner, Harold Taylor (ACU), Alex Scobie, Neale Shilton, Len Bayliss, Tyrell Smith, Bob Manns, Allan Jefferies, Ernie Nott, M.Deleport (Dunlop), Jim Alves.

Len Bayliss at speed on the Montlhéry banking.

Scene in the 'pits' at Montlhéry. Len Bayliss leaning on the ladder, Tyrell Smith, Ernie Nott writing, Harold Taylor, rep of Triumph France, Edward Turner looking thoughtful.

Allan Jefferies comes in for re-fuelling.

Alex Scobie refuels. Bob Holliday, Editor of Motor Cycling, on right (with hat).

Shilton gets the signal ready.

Shilton puts his signal to good use of the last lap.

After it is all over, congratulations from the Managing Director. Smiles all round.

For the record, the speeds attained, with allowance made for all stops, re-fuelling, change of riders etc were as follows :-

No 1 Machine – 92.23 mph
No 2 Machine – 92.48 mph
No 3 Machine – 92.33 mph

Including stops, the speeds were 90.30, 90.93 and 86.07 mph respectively.

After this, the three machines covered flying laps of the circuit at over 100 mph and the next day were ridden back to Meriden to be greeted by the BBC and the factory personnel, who turned out in force. Only two slight mishaps occurred during the whole operation. No 3 machine suffered a split tank, which was replaced, and a chainguard worked loose on the same bike which was removed. Incidentally, Edward Turner was a sharp eyed spectator in the 'pits' at Montlhéry, through most of the run.

These performances are all the more remarkable when it is borne in mind that the fuel used was the notorious war-time 'Pool', 72 octane, which permitted a compression ratio of only 7 to 1. Also, as an interesting comparison with today's superbikes, the Thunderbirds with spring wheel rear suspension weighed 385 lbs and cost £212.12.8 including purchase tax.

On the way home they just had to stop here for a picture.

Edward Turner explains what it is all about to David Martin of the BBC. The purpose of the whole operation is publicity.

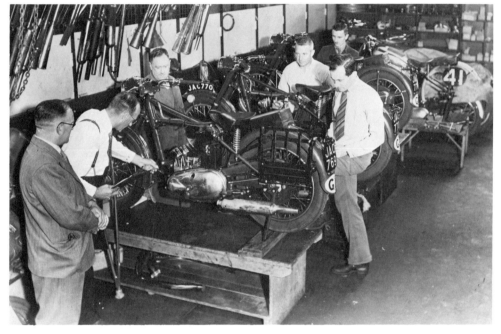

Back at the works the machines are stripped for examination by Harold Taylor, Dennis Hardwicke of Motor Cycling looks on. He reported that apart from a dry slack primary chain on JAC 770 'all three machines ... looked capable of an immediate repeat performance'.

When a new product is launched, the aim should be to have that new product in the dealers' shops on the morning of the launch in sufficient numbers to produce a lot of business. Very simple. But how often does this happen? I have been involved in many launches where the catalogues have been produced, the advertising has appeared, the press conferences have been held but not a single model was to be seen in the showrooms. All sorts of things can happen to produce this negative result, suppliers default, snags are met in production and so on. Unfortunately, once you have set the publicity bandwagon rolling it cannot be stopped very easily. Strikes, of course, can cause disaster. I recall one launch where the press went on strike that day so all our anticipated press mentions failed to materialise.

However, nothing went adrift with the Thunderbird launch. I seem to remember a figure of 2500 machines were built and ready at the time of the Montlhéry demonstration. Mind you, it did not pose too many problems for the works. The Speed Twin was in full production and the Thunderbird only called for bigger holes in the barrel with pistons to match, a modified crank and a different coat of paint. This may be oversimplifying it, but this was the very clever part of the whole operation – we got a new model, more performance and bigger profits for virtually peanuts.

I am happy to be able to record that one of the original Montlhéry Thunderbirds, JAC 769, is still around today. Many years after, I bought it back from its owner and it was restored in the works and subsequently loaned to the National Motor Museum at Beaulieu.

The other demonstration to which I referred as taking place in 1953 concerned a model very much at the bottom end of the range – the 'Terrier'. This was an interesting little 150cc ohv, an attempt by the factory to provide a sporting alternative to the run-of-the-mill lightweight two-stroke of the day. It was followed closely by a 200cc version, the 'Tiger Cub', which outlasted the Terrier as this disappeared after 1956. I recall the first prototype Terrier to be built, it was completed late one afternoon and the grapevine said it would be fired up that evening for the first time. We all contrived to stay late and sure enough the experimental boys duly appear–with their new baby (it really was a baby). They started kicking...and kicking...and kicking...nothing happened. 'Let's give it a push' they said, so we did, all of us, in turn. Up and down the gangway alongside the assembly track we galloped, but not a squeak could we get out of it. It was not a case of 'back to the drawing board' but it certainly went back to the experimental and next day the problem, whatever it had been, was solved and the little four-stroke ran very sweetly and everyone around had a ride.

To get back to the demo, again all sorts of ideas were thrown up and in the case of the Terrier the virtues that needed to be demonstrated were reliability and economy. Speed was not important in a 150 designed for the ride-to-worker. In the end the scheme agreed was certainly different, even if the route was not. It was that old favourite, Lands End to John O'Groats. Three bikes were to be used but it was the riders that caused a stir. They were to be Edward Turner himself (52), Bob Fearon, Works Director (46) and Alec Masters, Service Manager (56). Alec was a remarkable character who rode a bike to work every day and had an inexhaustable fund of stories and adventures that earned him great popularity on the club speaker circuit. He was an authority on the workings of a Triumph, needless to say, and was the author of several books. He also introduced me to my wife-to-be, Doreen, who worked in his Service Office at Warwick during the war and later at Meriden, when the new factory was commissioned. We married in 1948, much to the astonishment of colleagues, who had no idea that there was a romance going on in their midst – we were very discreet.

Bob Fearon was an ex-BSA man and his bluff good humour made him a popular figure. Although he had not ridden a motorcycle for some years, he was ready to have a go on this mission and confessed afterwards that he had enjoyed every minute.

Motor Cycling christened this run, very aptly, 'The Gaffers Gallop'. The plan was to ride from Lands End to John O'Groats, plus some additional mileage, to bring the total up to 1000 miles and the average speed was to be 30 mph. The whole operation would be under ACU supervision.

The first thing was to kit out the riders, Masters was no problem as he rode every day, but Turner and Fearon had to invest in new Barbour suits, boots, helmets, the lot. Finally, on 5th October, after a press reception at the factory, the riders moved off at around 1 pm, en route for Lands End, stopping overnight at Exeter. Next day they made for Bodmin where the run officially started – between here and Lands End was the extra mileage mentioned earlier.

The run proceeded very smoothly, according to plan, and even the weather was kind right

The 'Gaffers Gallop'; the three intrepid riders about to leave the works for Lands End. The factory turns out in support.

Three smiling 'Gaffers' prepare to set off on the long haul to John O'Groats.

*A re-fuelling stop. The ACU steward, John McNulty, keeps a **very** close watch on the proceedings.*

Led by Alec Masters, the three riders put in some stylish cornering.

*Three serious riders some-
where in Scotland. Alec
Masters ignores the white
line.*

*One of the overnight halts was Leamington Spa (maybe because the Managing Director lived close by?).
Here the riders look happy, supported by Eric Headlam, chief organiser and John McNulty, ACU
Steward.*

Safely arrived at John O'Groats with the picture to prove it. Bob Fearon on the left, Edward Turner in the centre and Alec Masters on the right.

up to the last day, Saturday 10th October, when some rain fell. So almost did Bob Fearon, who ran out of road on one bend, took to the grass and hit a concealed culvert. How he stayed on was a miracle, but he regained the road and the observers following behind breathed again.

When the results were computed, the machines had averaged 36.68 mph and 108.6 mpg, which was comfortably in excess of the target figures of 30 mph and 100 mpg. For 150cc machines carrying riders weighing 14 st 3 lbs, 16 st 7lbs and 13 st 7lbs this was very satisfactory and the point had been made. In 1911 Ivan B. Hart-Davies with his 500cc single gear Triumph had averaged 30.34 mph, an interesting contrast.

At first glance these demonstrations look fairly simple and straightforward to organise but this is not usually the case and many weeks of hard work go into them. Take the Montlhéry run by the Thunderbirds, for instance. The logistics of getting four motorcycles with their riders across the Channel does not seem too difficult but when you realise that in those days there were no sponsors with fat cheque books to pay for back-up trucks and fleets of cars and that the actual motorcycles being used in the demonstration also had to be used for transporting all the gear, things take on a very different complexion. If you look at the photograph of the bikes leaving Meriden you will see that they are heavily laden and two of the riders even have spare tyres slung round them. They rode back to Meriden the same way too which, if it did nothing else, proved that the motorcycles were perfectly normal, tractable road-going machines

Looking at the 'Gaffers Gallop' schedule, this was timed to a minute for arrival and departure at lunch and tea stops, hotels had to be booked and petrol supplies ensured at the right places, based on tank size and anticipated consumption. As the Managing Director was one of the riders, any slip-up was unthinkable.

Close up of the Terrier engine, the general concept of which was used in a whole range of single cylinder engines by both Triumph and BSA some years later.

The 150cc Triumph Terrier, introduced in 1953. This particular example was one prepared for the Earls Court Motor Cycle Show. It has the Terrier logo in gold on the front number plate and is very highly polished.

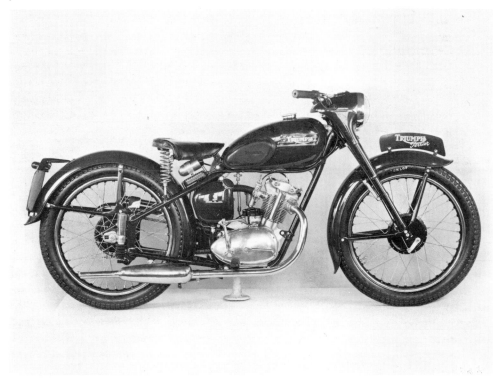

The Terriers were assembled in exactly the same way as the big machines, but they had their own track.

However good the demonstration, it is a complete waste of time unless it results in some favorable publicity. This all has to be organised beforehand and in the case of the 'Gaffers Gallop' our press agent, Reeves Quann, went along and made sure that the local press en route knew all about it. In every case they had been alerted some days before and a reporter was usually waiting. The riders were described in the handout as 'The man who designed it, the man who made it and the man who will service it'. This was a nice little gimmick which produced a lot of column inches up and down the country. Dealers on the route had all been warned some time before and were able to set up special displays in their windows to tie up with the local publicity that the run was getting.

In later years, when production racing became established, the need for these demonstrations declined. First the Bonneville and then the Trident proved in the Isle of Man and elsewhere that Triumph was very hard to beat, which is really what it is all about.

On Brooklands Track

PHOTO BY "THE MOTOR CYCLE"

Pre-war Maudes Trophy attempt. Two machines, a Speed Twin and a Tiger 100, covered 2350 miles under ACU observation which included 6 hours on Brooklands track where they averaged 75 and 78.5 mph respectively. The riders here on Brooklands are Allan Jefferies and Ivan Wicksteed. The Trophy was duly won.

Chapter Sixteen

Testers at work

Before the days of the 'Rolling Road' a small army of testers was employed by every factory to make sure that the product was as near perfect as possible before it reached its ultimate owner. The usual procedure was to take a bike as it came off the track, check that everything worked, put some fuel and oil in and take it for a run on the road. This usually lasted about fifteen to twenty minutes, after which it was then returned to the works and any adjustments necessary were carried out. If there was anything seriously wrong it would go to 'Rectification' for attention. Testing was a responsible job and the testers were a dedicated band of enthusiasts. It was a job much sought after and just as many young lads dreamed of being engine drivers so young motorcyclists often imagined the testers life to be their idea of heaven. To do what they loved doing, ride motorcycles, and get paid for it seemed too good to be true. But the testers lot was not always a happy one (like the policeman in the song). He had to go out wet or fine, usually over the same dreary route, day in day out, on the same sort of machines. He had a fiddling little card to fill in when he got back and he could not write because his fingers were blue with the cold. The foreman was bad tempered, trying to keep his testers ahead of the track, and even if he reported a fault, he knew no one would take any notice because 'they're all like that'. What a life!

Occasionally things go really wrong in the testers day. We had a dealer once who rang up to complain that a bike we had delivered to him was minus one gear, it had only three. No one believed him of course but he insisted, so to placate him the offending bike was brought back to the works. The dealer was right, it did have only three gears. Stripping the box revealed a faulty camplate. The big mystery was how did it get past the testers? So the records were checked and tester 'A' had signed it off as OK. So a plot was hatched and the machine was fed through the system again, still with the defective camplate, and so organised that it fell to tester 'A' to have to test it again, he not being aware of the 'plot'. Out he went, back he came,

Testers are not always good actors. A very posed picture of three of them round a unit Tiger 100.

card filled in all correct. He had missed it again. Needless to say he was moved off testing that very day. But it did prove how monotonous and automatic testing could become – to such an extent that a major malfunction went unnoticed.

Occasionally the monotony is relieved when someone in the office wants a letter or package delivered to some distant destination that very day. An urgent part for delivery to a dealer or a sample for a supplier. 'Send for a tester' is the cry and some lucky lad has a nice ride at high velocity to Manchester, or London or Southampton. Nothing better if the weather is fine.

'Immaculate white overalls' – three testers leaving the works to show the flag at some big local parade.

These Triumph testers are engaged in passing out Model H machines for the British Army, hence the armbands. Third on the left is Triumph road racer, George Shemans.

Here's a fine body of men, all set to test a big batch of Mr. Sykes' Model X 174cc two strokes. What, no helmets?

And you thought that 'wheelies' were a modern invention. You should try it with a belt drive model 'H'.

Another job testers get occasionally is to take part in some local function, where a motorcycle escort is required. Dressed in immaculate white overalls, usually with a Triumph badge on the pocket, a dozen testers look splendid escorting the Lord Mayor and it is good publicity for the firm. The only problem is that these jobs often entail riding at five miles an hour or less, which can be very hard on the clutch of a rorty twin.

Testers are truly a breed on their own and you will rarely find one who would like to do something different. They are still employed today, of course, but not in such large numbers and their job is to test sample machines off the track almost to destruction. They cover very high mileages and bring back vital information on what happens to the product after 10 or 20,000 miles. Some gifted testers have the ability to say *why* a machine is misbehaving. They can all say that it snakes at 80 but very few can pinpoint the reason and to a designer a man with this ability is worth his weight in gold.

When Triumph Engineering started up at the Priory Street works in 1936, they inherited an incredible vintage character who had survived from the belt drive days, through the 'Ricardo' years and in 1936 was still responsible for testing customers' machines which had been attended to in the works repair shop. His name was Lamb and he was known affectionately as 'Lammy'. But it was his attire that caught the eye. He wore leather leggings and knee breeches, a flat 'Coventry' cap (complete with button on top), a dilapidated pair of goggles and a unique belt which sported a leather tool bag. From this he would proudly produce his jet reamers (Turner's comment was 'Heaven forbid') and a small bulb horn or at any rate a bulb from which the horn had fallen off long since. He looked exactly like Bruce Bairnsfather's 'Old Bill' of Great War fame, looking for a better 'ole – or as if he had just retreated from Mons. Nevertheless, he knew his motorcycles and must have made a very considerable contribution over the years. He disappeared from the new Triumph scene before many months had elapsed, leather jerkin, moustache and all – so maybe he had found his better 'ole.

The power of these old bikes is fantastic, you just can't keep the front wheel down.

Army inspectors check their purchases very closely but even so the bikes have to be tested in the normal way, as well. TRW's leaving the Meriden factory on a test run.

Testers do go out in all weathers but there are limits. Reg Ballard posed this one for us many years ago.

Like so much modern technology there is no romance about the Rolling Road. It does the job coldly, efficiently and swiftly — and it doesn't miss gears — but the world is a poorer place without the likes of dear old 'Lammy'.

Alex Scobie, one of Triumph's best known testers. Long distances at high speed were Alex's speciality and it was obvious that he would be enlisted as one of the riders for the Thunderbird demonstration at Montlhéry in 1949, where this shot was taken.

Chapter Seventeen

Report on Japan

In 1960 when the threat of Japanese competition was making itself felt, Edward Turner paid a visit to that country to get some idea of the size and scope of this threat. The report he wrote on his return is reprinted here in full.

To those who posed the question 'Why did you not do something about the Japanese?' the answer is long and complex but having read this report, no one can say that we were not warned.

26th September, 1960.

REPORT ON JAPAN.
by
Edward Turner

As a result of the tremendous growth of the Japanese motor cycle Industry and the world-wide repercussions on our industry, it was decided that I should pay a visit to Japan to see first-hand what is going on, to examine if possible their organisations, to visit the principal factories, to observe manufacturing methods, to discuss with Japanese Managements their plans, particularly as regards export and to obtain as much information as possible on the Japanese motor cycle Industry in order that we should be fully informed of the situation and be in a position to plan counter measures to try and preserve our own share in the motorcycle world markets.

I had previously examined one or two of the better Japanese products such as the Yamaha, Honda and Suzuki, and formed a very high opinion of their design, finish and manufacturing accuracy, but no impression I had gained of the obvious upsurge of this important industry in Japan bore any relation to the shocks I received on closer examination of this situation on their home ground.

The revelations of Japan as a whole are truly shocking and I am amazed that more has not been published in those British national newspapers purporting to keep the public of this country informed of world developments.

Japan has 90 million highly intelligent, very energetic, purposeful people, all geared to an economic machine with an avowed object of becoming great again, this time in the world of business and industry, and nothing apparently is going to stop them. Tokyo with its population of 11 millions, the largest city in the world, is entirely Western and the streets are crammed with well-dressed, well-behaved busy people. Its traffic congestion, composed almost entirely of Japanese cars and motorcycles, is as bad as in any other city of the world but over a much greater area, and the shops and great stores are filled with an infinite variety of goods, all of the highest quality.

At the outset one must discard the old concept of Japanese manufacture being a cheap imitation of that of the West. To-day with Japanese manufactured goods of all types, the accent is on quality. They are fully aware of the reputation they have to live down and for many years now the finest machine tool equipment, techniques and scientific ability and keen commercial enterprise have been applied to this end.

Japan to-day is the largest manufacturer in the world of motorcycles, all of excellent quality. One company of this largest national producer of motorcycles produces more motorcycles than the whole of the British Industry put together and this is only one of the 20 or more motorcycle companies in full operation. They are producing well over half a million motorcycles a year (against 140,000 British), of which Honda produces approaching a quarter of a million, with 5 other companies each producing more than 25,000 units a year.

The production of motorcycles has been accelerating so fast that it is very difficult to obtain up-to-date figures of the current output but in every case it can be assumed to be more rather than less the figures stated in Appendix A. The reason for this tremendous upsurge in motorcycle manufacture (which, incidentally, has been occurring in the camera, radio and domestic appliance industries with equal intensity and similar rates of acceleration) is the very high standard of living enjoyed by the Japanese population to-day, brought about by the peculiar living conditions in Japan, where personal overheads are low, and although wages are also low by our standards the margin for spending is probably greater than in our own country. The motorcycle business is exactly suited to the improved conditions of young Japan and young Japan regards a motorcycle, purchased mostly on instalments, as being a desire-able acquisition from a transportation point of view and gaining "face". Also Japan has become since the war very much a mechanical and technical nation. The great wealth that poured into Japan as a result of Occupation and the relatively small proportion of the Budget being devoted to Defence until recent times, together with the very liberal approach to industry of Japanese financiers, have been of course major causes for what can only be described as a phenomenon.

I see the Japanese to-day combining the intense conscientious thoroughness and meticulous attention to detail of the German, with a very open-handed uninhibited approach to sales of the most blatant American sales corporation. This combination, together with a restless energy and a national sense of purpose, has had spectacular results in the nation's economy. Of course there have been casualties and in the motorcycle business many firms have gone under and many more are likely to follow. I see clearly the bigger fish swallowing the smaller ones and although I would not be surprised to see less than 10 motorcycle companies in existence in three years' time, 4 or 5 of these 10 will be immensely powerful.

The speed with which the Japanese motorcycle companies can produce new designs and properly tested and developed models is startling and the very large scientific and technical staff maintained at the principal factories is of course out of all proportion to anything ever visualised in this country, or for that matter in the United States. Honda alone, the largest company, has an establishment of 400 technicians engaged in studying new manufacturing techniques, new designs, new developments and new approaches. The whole of the technical and scientific force of Japan which enabled them, without help, to put up such a considerable show in the last war and a whole new generation of young scientists seem to have flocked to the motorcycle, motor car and electronic industries, and unlike our own country there is an enormous pool of well-trained brains to be had at nominal cost.

Wages of course are, by our standards, very low. The Yamaha Company for instance, which is an old-established musical instrument firm making pianos, harmonicas, etc, were not in the motorcycle business five years ago and their progress is dramatic in that they have a well-equipped factory twice the size of Triumph with a first-class product and are currently making over 80,000 units a year. They pay only £10 per month, reckoning 1000 Yens to the £. Honda pay rather more and would average £15 per month, but it should be borne in mind that the system is different from ours. The work-people live in company-owned houses and pay less than a dollar a month rent and buy food at cost.

On the other hand, there is no question in Japan of laying off workpeople. When an industrial enterprise employs people, it keeps them on the payroll through good times and bad, but the disadvantage of this situation for them will be apparent only in bad times. There are still two to three million unemployed in Japan, notwithstanding its very busy economy. The newspapers claim this figure but the Government only admits to 300,000, but all appear to be prosperous in the outlying cities through which I passed on the way to Hamamatsu, which is one of the big motorcycle centres some 250 miles from Tokyo. I noticed particularly people waiting on the railway stations as I passed through; they were well dressed in Western style and seemed to be more prosperous than the people of many provincial towns in this country to-day.

I visited the Yamaha, Suzuki and Honda factories, was well received and shown anything I cared to see. My sponsors, the Triumph distributors Messrs. Mikuni Shoko, are a Japanese company with a hook-up with Amal in this country, and apart from the relatively unimportant side of their business of handling imported motorcycles, they are large carburetter manufacturers supplying carburetters to the motorcycle and motor car industry in quite a big way.

They assigned their Import Manager to look after me during my journey but unfortunately he spoke only limited English and, therefore, I was at some disadvantage in going into real technicalities or any subtleties of polite conversation. On the other hand, I felt I had the advantage of a better reception by being in the company of a Japanese.

During the time I was away from Tokyo on these visits, I stayed in Japanese style hotels, which though elegant and interesting, are by Western standards not the most comfortable in the world.

YAMAHA: At their factory I saw a shop floor scene not very dissimilar from Triumph but with far more movement, particularly of components, a certain amount of mechanisation and a high tempo of good quality and apparent enthusiastic effort. Machine tool equipment was first-class and new.

In common with the other two factories I visited, 85% of the machine tools were Japanese made and the odd 15% were split up between German, Swiss and American. The only piece of British equipment I saw used was Sykes gear cutters, of which they spoke highly.

SUZUKI: The Suzuki factory, reputed to be the second largest to Honda, was previously engaged entirely in the manufacture of weaving machines, looms, etc. and went into the motorcycle business after the war with great profit. The principals had visited Triumph in this country which put me on rather a better basis for discussion. They were courteous and willing to discuss any aspect of their business with me. Their factory was even more mechanised than that of Yamaha and very self-contained, making its own castings, forgings, presswork, etc.

HONDA: The last factory I visited was Honda. This particular factory was only three years old, up to the minute, being windowless, air-conditioned and designed specifically for the purpose of efficient motorcycle production. The Hamamatsu factory is one of two, the other being outside Tokyo, with a third in process of being built and equipped at the cost of over £6,000,000. The chief of operations at Honda was Mr. Honda, the younger brother of the President, who was very pleasant, frank and courteous. Mr. Honda expressed great respect and admiration for the British Motor Cycle Industry and felt that though some of our products were old fashioned, he was not deceived by this as he thought the "C" Range of Triumph (350 c.c./500 c.c.) were equally up-to-date in comparison with anything being made in Japan. This is our latest range introduced three years ago.

The Honda factory was everything that one could desire as an up-to-date manufacturing conception for motorcycles, and although nothing I saw was beyond our conception or ability to bring about in our own factories, it should be borne in mind that we have not now nor ever have had, the quantities of any one product which would justify these highly desirable methods being used. They had a large number of single-purpose, specially designed machine tools which reduce labour for any large component, such as the crankcase, to an absolute minimum. All components, except very small ones such as gear shafts and gears more conveniently transported in trays, were moving on conveyors throughout the factory. Every section for the small, medium and larger motorcycles being made was geared to a time cycle, all assembly was on moving bands. Paint and chrome was of high quality from automatic plants. The chrome, though not as good as we produce in our industry, was apparently entirely without polishing, being coppered nickel and bright chrome on all the large components, with quite tolerable finish. The surface finishes of machined parts and standards of accuracy were, I should think, better than our best work and most complex and elaborate equipment was used throughout on gauging, all developed in Japan.

Although their wages are roughly speaking a quarter of ours, they were nevertheless extremely economical in the use of manpower. Apart from assembly, I saw very little handwork except for the odd frazing of castings to ensure they fitted spotting fixtures without trouble.

Engine and machine assembly was moving and all the components seem to go together consistently and without difficulty, as indeed they had to in order to maintain the timed stations.

Testing in all factories was done on rollers geared to brakes which gave horsepower readings while the machine was stationary. A final run round the test track within the factory seemed to suffice to ensure the roadworthy standards.

Edward Turner with Mr Benjiro Honda during his visit to Japan. When this photograph was taken Mr Benjiro Honda (brother of 'Mr Honda') was general manager of the Hamamatsu factory and a main board director.

Packing of various kinds was very slick, with numerous tracks coming and going to take away the merchandise.

The whole was a dynamic experience and a somewhat frightening spectacle.

The capital investment in these factories is of course enormous and they are all self-contained, making their own iron and aluminium castings, forgings and, particularly, pressings. Their toolroom was very large, well manned and extremely busy, with elaborate and brand-new press equipment.

There was no colour variation as far as I could see other than chrome and black but one or two specials were made for racing purposes in batches of 20.

They told me that they could see a reduction in the rate of acceleration of output for the home market and that they were, therefore, concentrating more on world markets.

When I returned to Tokyo finally a meeting was arranged by Messrs. Mikuni Shoko, my hosts as it were, for the Trade, Press and one or two University professors to meet me and I was asked if I would submit myself to questioning after giving them a short address on the purpose of my visit. I naturally agreed to this and a highly placed official of practically every principal company attended, together with the national and technical Press and one or two scientists including the President of the Tokyo University. They paid me, as a representative of the British Motor Cycle Industry, considerable respect and were kind enough to say that they acknowledged the great work that the U.K. had done during the last 50 years in the Motor Cycle Industry. They felt, however, that Japan afforded a unique opportunity for the Motor Cycle Industry by virtue of the substantial prosperity now being enjoyed and the great interest of young Japan in mechanical transportation.

It should be borne in mind that the Motor Car Industry in Japan also is enjoying a great boom and to give some idea of their approach, an Austin car is being made under licence in one factory and selling only 500 a month but they have duplicated the complete automation of Longbridge even for these quantities, and I am bound to say the product is even better finished than that of this country. It should be clearly remembered that Japan is no longer copying Western products, apart from odd examples such as this. They are designing from first principals on the most scientific, logical and commercial basis and the whole gamut of so-called Western manufactured products in the automotive, electronic and domestic appliance fields is being pursued on an entirely original basis with many new techniques and inventive approaches. I understand the optical business, for which Germany has long been famous, is far surpassed both in quality and price by Japan, and in radio it is well known that they lead the world for price and quality in the transistor field, tape recorders, etc.

It may appear by this report that I am inclined to emphasise and exaggerate but I am purposely avoiding any form of exaggeration. It is essential that our industry in general and the B.S.A. Group in particular should know the facts and what we are up against in the retention of our export markets. Even our home market for motorcycles will be assailed and although personally I do not think the Japanese Motor Cycle Industry will eclipse the traditional type of machine that the British motorcyclist wants and buys, they are bound to make some impact on our home market by virtue of the high quality of their product and low prices.

Having familiarised myself with the situation as it exists I have been giving considerable thought to what we might do, and a course to pursue to combat this situation, and I must confess that these answers are going to be hard to find. In the first place it should be borne in mind that the Motor Cycle Industry has never been big business in Britain. Its safety has to some extent been that it has never attracted big capital and big enterprise. We have never made to date, even in these relatively boom times, 1,000 units of any one product in a week consistently, whereas many factories in Japan are currently doing this in a day. It is true that many of the large quantities in Japan are on small motorcycles but even the larger ones (250 c.c./300 c.c.) are being turned out in quantities in excess of any equivalent model in this country and, therefore, it has never been feasible – and certainly not economically sound – to lay down manufacturing lines fully mechanised with complete single-purpose machine tool equipment of special design at every stage of manufacture.

Experience has shown that the British Motor Cycle Industry and our many export markets abroad want a range of motorcycles from each manufacturer. It may well be that we have not had the courage to reduce our variety of manufacture so as to produce larger requirements for any given model but previous attempts in this direction have always led to a reduction in overall turnover. Therefore, with Japan they have the manifold advantages of a large requirement for a single, developed article and they have had the great courage to invest enormous sums of money with full confidence that their products will be purchased in sufficient quantities at home and abroad, and currently they are in full flight and are receiving snowball advantages from their enterprise.

I pointed out to the meeting that Britain having opened up its doors to Japanese motorcycles, it is only fair that Japanese Trade should agree to similar measures for British machines and in any case, as far as I could see, they had nothing to lose. Although this remark registered and there is some talk of liberalising British imports of motorcycles next spring, it is not thought by our importers that this will happen and even if it did, in my judgment it would not result in the British Motor Cycle Industry participating significantly in the large Japanese home market owing to a very large price disparity. My thoughts are entirely directed towards the preservation of our existing export markets on which our companies depend to the tune of from 30% to 40% of our output (Triumph 49%, B.S.A. 35%, Ariel insignificant abroad as yet).

One of the most practical thoughts in this present situation would be to visualise opening up our own motorcycle operations in Japan, thereby obtaining the full advantages of their plentiful and cheap labour and having available a window for observation on the Japanese Industry. We might even, should we consider this, obtain technical help which is not to be despised, particularly in regard to our future tooling and development.

By and large the menace of Japanese motorcycles to our own export markets is that they are producing extremely refined and well finished motorcycles up to 300 c.c. at prices which reach the public at something like 20% less. The machines themselves are more comprehensive than our own in regard to equipment, such as electrical starting, traffic indicators, etc., are probably better made but will not appeal to the sporting rider to anything like the same extent as our own. However, they will make very big inroads into the requirement for motorcycles for transportation.

On scooters, due to the poor roads of Japan, which follow a pattern of being relatively good surface for reasonable distances, terminated by a series of very bad potholes, the smaller wheeled scooter is not gaining favour. There are, however, a number of quite good scooters made but I do not regard this aspect as being too serious at this stage.

Note: There were two appendices, one giving Japanese production figures for the first half of 1960 and the second stating the implications and what was involved if a manufacturing operation in Japan was thought worthy of consideration.

Chapter Eighteen

In conclusion

Triumph has had many ups and downs in its long history and this book has been concerned mainly with one of the 'up' periods which started with the formation in 1936 of the Triumph Engineering Co Ltd. From this point, over the next thirty years, it was built up into an immensely successful and prosperous company. Its products sold in great numbers in all parts of the world, particularly in the United States, which developed into a vast motorcycle market, and it would not be an exaggeration to claim that it was Triumph that sparked this market off in the immediate post war years.

Triumph was an unusual company in many ways in those days. It inspired great loyalty from its employees and the senior management remained virtually unchanged for a great many years. The Directors were good pickers of men and knew how to train and mould them into the company way of life — a way of life in which no one suffered from delusions of grandeur. Procedures were often homespun but efficient nevertheless, and pennies were not spent if halfpennies would do the job. These good days passed away when Edward Turner retired and closer integration with BSA followed.

The past ten years have been frustrating ones for Triumph and one cannot help speculating that things might have gone a lot better if Triumph had not joined the BSA Group way back in 1951. Jack Sangster himself put this view forward to me at the height of the recent troubles and there is a lot to be said for it. This is not to disparage our good friends up the road at Small Heath with whom I worked very happily for a number of years before returning to Meriden. But Big is not always Better and the rationalisation between the two companies never worked and only brought on worse problems later. We might both have been better off pursuing our separate ways in happy competition.

However it is no good crying over spilt milk and Triumph still had some great days to come in the seventies when the howl of the Trident was heard in the land. This was surely the most evocative sound heard on the race tracks since the Scotts of early days.

In the Picture Gallery which follows this note, I have included a selection of Trident racing shots even though they may appear to be out of period with the rest of the book. But are they? Apart from the fact that the Trident three cylinder engine was a logical development by Bert Hopwood and Doug Hele of Edward Turner's vertical twin, surely the Trident was the final fling of the old Triumph spirit of supremacy, a flash of brilliant sunshine before the storm clouds closed over — temporarily we hope.

Ivor Davies

207

Picture Gallery

Bird's eye view of the alloy 'Delta- head introduced for the T110 and TR6 in 1956 in single carburetter form and as a twin carburetter optional extra for the Tiger 100 a year later.

'A thing of beauty —' the 1951 all-alloy Tiger 100 engine. The fine pitch fins add a distinctive touch to this splendid engine.

The handsome chromed tank badge introduced in 1957 replacing the four parallel bands which came in with the 'Thunderbird' in 1949.

The Tigress Scooter which could be bought with either a 250cc ohv twin engine or a 175cc two-stroke. Introduced at the tail-end of the fifties, they completely failed to loosen the Italian stranglehold on the scooter market.

In 1962 the Tina lightweight scooter came out with its ingenious automatic transmission using a belt on expanding and contracting pulleys. The engine was a 100cc two-stroke and the slogan was 'No gears, no clutch, goes at a touch'. A couple of years later an updated version known as the T10 came along as illustrated here. But the scooter boom was over.

The very neat little 250 ohv engine and transmission unit of the Tigress. Wheels were attached on one side only as on a car.

Prototype of a Triumph three-wheeler designed by Edward Turner in 1962. It used the 250cc ohv engine unit from the Tigress Scooter. It was reputed to be very unstable at speed and the project was hastily dropped.

Molly Briggs was a very well known competitor on Triumphs in the post war period. Here she is picking her way carefully past a fallen rival in the ISDT in Wales. **(Motor Cycling).**

THE TRIUMPH MANAGEMENT TEAM – 1950
Back Row L to R Alec Masters (Service), Jack Wickes (Design), Harry Holland (Export), Syd Tubb (Assembly), Eric Headlam (Sales), John McDonnell (Production), Neale Shilton (Sales), Tyrell Smith (Experimental), Frank Baker (Development), Ivor Davies (Publicity),
Front Row L to R Bert Coles (Works Manager), Bob Fearon (Works Director), Edward Turner (Managing Director), Alf Camwell (Works Director retired), Charles Parker (Director & Secretary), Ted Crabtree (Buyer), Jack Welton (Sales).

John Young Sangster Chairman and founder of Triumph Engineering, known affectionately as 'Mr Jack' or 'JYS'. This is a portrait possibly given to him on his retirement in 1961 as Chairman of the BSA Group when he handed the company over with record profits of £3,418,548. He died in 1977.

Herbert Hopwood, designer and engineer was with Edward Turner at Ariel, came with him to Triumph, moved to Norton after the war, then to BSA as Chief Engineer, back to Norton as director and finally returned to Triumph in the sixties. The Dominator, the Gold Star, the Golden Flash and the Trident all had Bert Hopwood's signature on them.

C.W.F.P.

With the greatest affection and regard from your associates at Triumph

C.W.F. Parker, Financial Director & Secretary. Held in great affection by all who worked with him. Loved high performance motorcycles, cars and steam locomotives. Knew where every penny went and kept the company in profit at all times. This cartoon was prepared on the occasion of his retirement.

216

Anthony Smith, author and broadcaster, walked into a dealer's shop in Cape Town, bought a secondhand Cub and rode it to Cairo!

Believe it or not, this bear, Lisa, was trained to ride a Tigress scooter, at Bertram Mills Circus.

Directors meet – Charles Parker and Bert Hopwood chat to Marilyn and Pete Colman at Earls Court. Colman, ex-racer, was a top man from the Triumph West Coast USA operation.

1957 marked the 21st birthday of the company and a dinner was organised at the Leofric Hotel in Coventry. Here, Edward Turner is receiving a presentation clock from Charles Parker.

Edward Turner sets up a nice picture with a 1940 Speed Twin and some pretty girls – in the USA, of course.

Well, after all, Edward Turner was Managing Director of the BSA Automotive Division at one time! The cheerful looking passenger is Bill Rawson, Sales Director of BSA Motor Cycles Ltd.

A post-war picture (with tele forks). The lady? None other than that star of the big screen, Rita Hayworth.

A serious looking group at the launch of the Tigress scooter in London. L to R Edward Turner, Stirling Moss, Jack Sangster and Lord Brabazon.

Lord Brabazon tries a Trophy TR6 for size, Edward Turner (and the author) in attendance. Lord Brabazon held the first pilot's licence issued in Britain. (Fox Photos).

Who's driving this thing? Stirling and Harry Secombe seem to have problems here.

Trust the Americans to devise the 'Sno-go' to fit lightweight motorcycles for riding in snow or sand. The long-suffering bike is a Cub.

Neale Shilton, motorcycle salesman extraordinary, on one of his mammoth trips abroad. Seen here with Buster Reinhardt, Triumph Danish distributor. Shilton is reputed to have covered a million miles on two wheels.

Triumph police customers spanned the world. This one was in the Bahamas nicely posed with a luxury liner on the horizon.

Taking the press out to lunch! L to R Cyril Quantrill ('Motor Cycling'), Ivor Davies, Neale Shilton, Jack Wickes and Bob Hakewell ('Motor Cycling').

The rather haughty camel meets a Triumph somewhere east of Suez.

Shots with animals are sometimes better than those with pretty girls for getting into the papers. This one originated in America, we believe.

The newly opened M6 motorway was an obvious place for a good police publicity shot.

A smart group from Ceylon in 1965. Crash helmets and bare knees are an odd combination.

228

This little detachment of Parisian motorcycle police helped us during the shooting of some hectic sequences for a Triumph film made in the fifties. It was entitled 'It's a Triumph'.

Rangoon, Burma. A posse of police on 500s with the famous Shwedagon Pagoda in the background.

B.J. Hargreaves after winning the Clubman's TT on a Tiger 100 in 1952. His average speed was 82.45 mph.

The evergreen Percy Tait on a Bonneville. His performances on road and track have become a part of the Triumph legend.

Norman Hyde with his monstrous blown Trident-engined dragster. Norman was development engineer on Tridents at the factory and holds the world speed record for sidecars at 161.8 mph set with a 831cc Trident.

A Rolling Road, the device that put paid to the employment of large numbers of testers. In fifteen minutes or so, all the vital information necessary to know whether a bike will function properly can be ascertained.

The Profile Projector, a useful instrument which enables you to see what a component really looks like. The actual valve can be seen in the vice on the platen below.

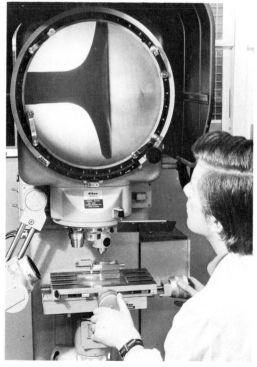

Two of Edward Turner's first motorcycles will be found elsewhere in this book; this is the last one he ever designed. It is a 350 ohc twin which became the 'Bandit' in the 1971 programme but was never made. The photograph is of the first prototype which is reputed to have been produced in three months and clocked 112 mph first time out. Note the mechanically-operated front disc brake.

This was Edward Turner's design for a motorcycle of the future. Produced as a large coloured painting by Jack Wickes, it now decorates a wall in the Coventry headquarters of the Motor Cycle Association.

Always a stickler for quality, Turner examines the silver candelabra given him by the BSA board as a retirement present. With him is the board chairman, Eric Turner (no relation).

The men behind the racing Tridents. L to R Bill Fannon, Arthur Jakeman, Jack Shemans, Fred Swift, Norman Hyde, Doug Hele and Les Williams. The bike on the right has a BSA label, that on the left a Triumph. They were virtually interchangeable and often were!

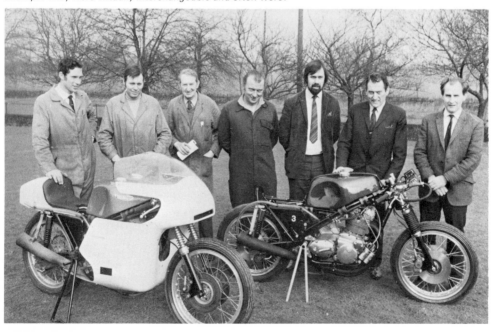

A corner of the 'race shop' at Meriden. Arthur Jakeman (in background), Jack Shemans (centre) and Fred Swift (foreground). A 1970 picture.

The frame of the 1970 racing Trident, light, simple and very strong.

Two views of the 1972 works racer. The neat engine and transmission layout can be seen in the unfaired shots.

Ray Pickrell aviating at Cadwell in 1972.

Tony Jefferies on his way to winning the 1973 Production TT on the legendary 'Slippery Sam'. This incredible machine, now the property of Les Williams, won the Production TT for five consecutive years – 1971/2/3/4/5. It also finished 4th in 1970!